No-Nonsense Leadership

Nadia van der Vlies

No-Nonsense Leadership

How to Become an Effective Leader, Manager and Coach

Warden Press

© 2019 Nadia van der Vlies, Amsterdam

ISBN:
Paperback: 978-94-92004-80-2
E-book (Epub): 978-94-92004-81-9
E-book (Kindle): 978-94-92004-82-6

Original title: *No-nonsense leidinggeven. Hoe je effectief coachend leidinggeeft* (Amsterdam: Boom, 2018).
Translated from the Dutch by Erwin Postma, Malaga.
Cover design: Studio Jan de Boer, Amsterdam
Interior: André Gubbels, AG-Freelance-dtp, Groningen
Photo author: Silviya Sobaci Photography, Amsterdam

This edition published by Warden Press, Amsterdam

wardenpress.com

Table of contents

Introduction   9

1   No-Nonsense Leadership   11
1.1   Mature Leadership   11
1.2   The Mature Model in Communication   12
1.3   The Mother, the Macho, and the Mole   15
1.4   Dealing with Needs for Help   29
1.5   Summary   33

2   Leadership Skills   35
2.1   Situational Leadership   35
2.2   Taking Ownership   41
2.3   Keeping Your Eye on the Bigger Picture   47
2.4   Conversation Skills for Mature Leadership   48
2.5   Summary   54

3   Leader, Manager, Coach   57
3.1   The Roles of Leader, Manager, and Coach   58
3.2   Summary   61

4   Leader   63
4.1   Leader: Conveys the Mission, Vision, and Strategy   63
4.2   Leader: Knows and Shares the Company's Values   65
4.3   Leader: Motivates and Inspires   68
4.4   Summary   71

5	**Manager**	73
5.1	Manager: Translates Vision into Goals	73
5.2	Manager: Monitors and Reviews Results and Behavior	74
5.3	Manager: Assesses and Adjusts	83
5.4	Summary	90
6	**Coach**	93
6.1	Coach: Encourages Others to Find Their Own Solutions	94
6.2	Coach: Facilitates the Development of Others (Who Are Not Aware of the Coaching Need)	100
6.3	Coach: Facilitates the Development of Others (Who Are Aware of the Coaching Need)	104
6.4	Summary	116
7	**Reflexes**	119
7.1	What are Reflexes?	120
7.2	Common Intervention Reflexes in Leadership	121
7.3	Intervention as a Choice Instead of a Reflex	124
7.4	How to Deal With These (Sometimes Awkward) Reflexes	125
7.5	Summary	126
8	**Tricky Situations**	127
8.1	Transactional Analysis	127
8.2	TA in Interaction	129
8.3	A Passive Employee	131
8.4	A Defiant Employee	133
8.5	A Moaning Employee	135
8.6	A Popular But Underachieving Employee	138
8.7	A Poorly Performing Employee	140
8.8	A Top-Performing Employee	141
8.9	A Sickly Employee	143
8.10	A Stressed Employee	145
8.11	An Emotional Employee	147
8.12	Quarreling Employees	149
8.13	Handling Your Own (Difficult) Manager	151
8.14	Summary	153

Bonus 1: The Truisms of No-Nonsense Leadership   155

1. To reflect = to learn   155
2. TheAnswer to most questions is 'let's talk about it'   155
3. If you have something to say, say it; if you have something to ask, ask it   155
4. If you work hard, the other won't have to   156
5. New behavior is acquired by doing, doing, and doing   156

Bonus 2: Glossary   157

Acknowledgments   165

Literature   167

Introduction

This book is intended for anyone who leads, manages, and coaches people or wants to know more about leading, managing, and coaching people, regardless of whether you are just starting out in a leadership role or already have years of leadership experience under your belt. I have taken widely accepted theory on leadership and psychology and translated it to everyday real-life situations.

My personal drive behind writing this book was that I myself would have liked to have had this kind of reference material when I started out leading teams. When, after over ten years in leadership, I entered a coaching program and learned that you can give others the responsibility to solve their own problems, it dawned on me that this is something that every manager should know. It ultimately inspired me to become a trainer myself, and it is why I enjoy training managers so much. I let them discover for themselves how to use coaching skills to get more out of their employees, and how to get their employees to take more responsibility. Taking more responsibility boosts employees' development, and it saves managers time and energy.

In the same way as we deliver trainings at NONONS, this book is practical, accessible, and clear. To illustrate my points, I use real-life examples from my own experiences or examples shared by managers I had in training groups, to make it much more relatable. You can instantly apply everything you read in this book in your day-to-day work, and perhaps even beyond your work life.

By no-nonsense leadership I basically mean 'let's not overcomplicate things.' There are plenty of books and theories that define leadership, but these books seldom describe HOW to actually do it, how to lead, manage, and coach people effectively. I know first-hand that many managers out there are looking for guidance and tools for effective leadership. How do you go about it, how do you get your employees to do what you want? And what do you do when things don't go your way? How do you address that and still make sure your employees stay motivated? ToAnswer these and other questions, I will start by looking at personal leadership, at the impact your behavior has on your employees. What works and what doesn't. What pitfalls to watch out for (Chapter 1). After that, the focus will shift to leadership skills (Chapter 2). I will describe the three different managerial roles of leader, manager, and coach (Chapter 3), detailing the duties, responsibilities, and skills that go with each of these three roles (Chapters 4 to 6). However, no matter how well you have got the theory down, your intervention reflexes can still get in the way (Chapter 7). In Chapter 8, you will read all about tricky situations and difficult employee types. Finally, at the back of the book, you will find a quick rundown of the truisms of non-nonsense leadership, as well as a glossary.

The basic goal of this book is to empower you, in all three of your roles, to choose your own behavior. To become aware not only of your attitude and the way you communicate, but also of the effects it has on others. And for this awareness to make you an even more effective leader, manager, and coach.

This book set in the context of management practices at organizations where managers are responsible for the performance of their teams. However, I do realize that there are also organizations these days that are switching to self-management, where the role of manager has all but disappeared. In practice, this means that all employees need skills you normally see in good managers, as employees in self-managing organizations need to challenge each other on behavior, assess each other's performance, and motivate each other. If you work in such a self-managing organization, you can read this book to explore which management duties and skills you would want to develop.

If you are committed to getting started with the insights and guidance from this book, you will find the assignments at the end of each chapter a great help. They will enable you to test your understanding of what you have just read and help you put it in practice. I realize I am stating the obvious, but the more time you devote to it, the more mindful you will become of your pitfalls and reflexes. And if changing proves tough going, you can always hire a coach or take coaching leadership training!

I hope you enjoy reading this book.

Nadia van der Vlies
NONONS Courses, Training and Coaching

Warning: you may be taken aback by some of the things you read about pitfalls and reflexes, because you recognize them from your personal experience and realize that you have walked into these pitfalls and had these reflexes. Perhaps reading this book leads you to doubt yourself and think, 'Am I doing it right?' Rest assured, it means you are on the right track. If you want to change, the first step is to get to the stage of conscious incompetence (see Section 6.3).

1 No-Nonsense Leadership

This first chapter is about giving your employees responsibility. Using a model that I have branded the *Mature Model*, I will show you the pitfalls you might encounter as a manager. Some of these pitfalls you may recognize, and some may loom larger than others in your day-to-day work. The fact is that you will be a much more effective manager if you are mindful of all these pitfalls and know what you can do to steer clear of them or get out of them. Let me start by explaining what I mean by 'mature.'

1.1 Mature Leadership

The word 'mature' takes us into the realm of 'adults.' My Mature Model is loosely based on Transactional Analysis (see Section 8.1), which distinguishes three different roles: the parent role, the adult role, and the child role.

In simple terms, the parent role is when you place yourself above the other, feeling that you have to take care of the other or tell the other how to do something. Section 1.3 will go into the parent role in greater detail, including different versions of it, such as the 'mother' role and the 'macho' role.

In the adult role, you take a slightly more detached approach to the situation, which allows you to identify what is going on between you and the other. This is when you take responsibility for yourself and assume that the other will be able to do the same. In other words, you believe that the other is capable enough to be able to perform his or her task and self-manage. This is what I call a mature attitude.

This mature attitude enables you to adopt a coaching leadership style. Just like a coach, you communicate with the other from a position of equality. You are not making yourself more important than the other, but not less important either. This means that you are able to help the other develop, as you make them personally responsible and empower them to come up with solutions. However, it also means that you honestly say what you think, feel, and believe.

What Does That Look Like, Mature Communication?

Imagine a co-worker comes to you with a problem and tells you she has no idea what to do. You, however, know exactly what she needs to do, and you help her on her way. Or imagine your manager asks you to write up a memo and you immediately say 'OK'. Later it dawns on you that writing memos is not part of your job description.

This chapter will show you that you have a choice. It will show you how to be driven less by must-dos or ought-to-dos. You can choose what to do. To get to that point, you need to detach yourself from the situation, because distance creates perspective.

The Core of a Coaching or Mature Leadership Style

By a coaching leadership style, I mean managing in mature mode. You have a choice. You can help your employee, but you can also decide not to. You can give pointers or comments, but you can also quiet. Having a mature leadership style means that you are able to reflect on the situation and make a conscious choice as to how to respond and what to do. This is when you align your behavior with what you think is needed or what would work for your employee, while always considering what is best for you, what is best for the other, and what is best for the company. It is communication based on equality, realizing and tapping into what is going on between you and your employee, which you are able to pinpoint in the here and now.

1.2   The Mature Model in Communication

When communicating with an employee, there are various possible positions you can adopt. If you want to take a coaching-based approach, you will do well to communicate from your mature position, as equals. That being said, this is far from easy to do. The Mature Model (see Figure 1.1) identifies three well-known pitfalls for managers: the macho role, the mother role, and the mole role. In an ideal world, you, as the manager, stay in mature mode most of the time. And you make a conscious choice to switch to the mother, macho, or mole role as and when required by the situation. Although there is nothing inherently wrong with these roles, the problem is that you (subconsciously) slip into them too often. And that is when they become pitfalls. In this chapter, I will offer stepping stones to help you consciously switch between roles. It will empower you to deliberately adopt certain behavior instead of responding on autopilot based on your usual reflex.

To establish a relationship of equals and help your employee take responsibility, there are two things you need to be able to do:

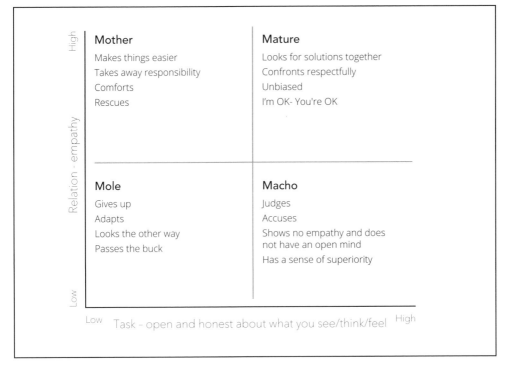

Mother	**Mature**	
Makes things easier	Looks for solutions together	
Takes away responsibility	Confronts respectfully	
Comforts	Unbiased	
Rescues	I'm OK- You're OK	
Mole	**Macho**	
Gives up	Judges	
Adapts	Accuses	
Looks the other way	Shows no empathy and does not have an open mind	
Passes the buck	Has a sense of superiority	

(Vertical axis: Relation - empathy, from Low to High)

(Horizontal axis: Low — Task - open and honest about what you see/think/feel — High)

Figure 1.1   The Mature Model

1. show empathy, take your employee's perspective, basically feeling with your employee without judging
2. not shy away from truthfully telling your employee what you have seen, what you think, and how you feel. This is all about addressing things that may be painful or sensitive

As soon as such talks become difficult, managers often tend to slip into a pitfall, sympathizing too much or being overly blunt or judgmental. The Mature Model shows how this works and what the effects are.

The Two Axes

The model is made up of two axes: the axis of empathy and the axis of being open and honest about what you see, think, and feel. A high score on both axes means that yours is a coaching mindset, which makes you a mature manager.

Many people think that a coaching leadership style and/or coaching itself is all about listening, regular uh-huhing and nodding to show that you are interested and going along with whatever the other has to say. Nothing could be further from the truth. True, a coaching manager needs to be a good listener and be able to truly engage with the other.

You basically need to be able to get into the other's head, so as to make your employee feel free enough to share his or her doubts and insecurities, to show vulnerability. A good coaching manager stands shoulder to shoulder with the employee, on the same level, without judging. But it is at least equally important to be able and dare to confront your employee. If you truly want your employee to develop, it is essential that you dare to challenge your employee on certain behavioral patterns. Behavior that you have seen from your employee in dealings with you or in interaction with others. In mature mode, you not only address behavior you have seen previously, but also behavior in the here and now, behavior your employee is showing during the conversation.

One of my employees likes to talk a lot, and she often fails to get to the point. I've noticed in myself that I sometimes dread talking to her. She told me once that she has ambitions to move into a senior role and would like to be consulted more by her co-workers. In a meeting with her, I explain what effect her excessive talking has on me, telling her that my mind tends to wander off. My tone in telling her this is friendly and not judgmental in any way. I'm telling her this to help her in her development. Friends and co-workers are unlikely to be this forthright with her about this. They will simply tune out and think about something else. Or they might joke about it with others.

Drawing her attention to this issue in an open and honest way is simply part of my job as a manager. If it leads to my employee realizing what effect her long-winded stories are having on others, she can become mindful of it and change her behavior.

The Manager's Attitude in Mature Mode
- *Equal.* You believe that you and your employee are equally entitled to feel comfortable. Your communication style accommodates both your and your employee's preferences.
- *You are unbiased.* You always try to keep your judgments to yourself. You show understanding and empathy.
- *You dare to address what is happening in the moment.* You are open and honest about what you notice and experience during the conversation with your employee. For example: when the conversation proves to be tough going, or you notice that you are getting irritated, you just come straight out with it. Or when you notice your employee's attention is drifting off, or your employee is overly modest, you openly share these perceptions with your employee. And you, ideally, do so in the moment, or as soon as possible after it.
- *You exude self-confidence.* You do not have a tendency to make yourself smaller than the employee. By that I mean that you do not efface yourself or adapt to your employee too much, but that you instead chart your own course.

- *You are open and vulnerable.* You do not have a tendency to make yourself bigger than the employee. You are open to other opinions and are functionally vulnerable. You do not hide the fact that you are not all-powerful and all-knowing, as you are only human, with doubts and concerns like anyone else.
- *Investigative and inquisitive.* You respond to resistance or hesitation with questions. You investigate the reasons behind your employee's behavior. You seek better understanding of your employee and try to figure out how to achieve more effective and engaging collaboration.
- *You inspire trust and are trusting.* You take responsibility, show a sense of direction in how you intend to get to where you want to go. This inspires trust and lets your employees know that they can rely on you. And you share responsibility, which shows that you have faith in your employees' talent. You give them space and freedom, so that they can take responsibility and grow.
- *You do not look for employees' appreciation.* You are not out to be liked by your employees. You want contact as equals.

In a coaching mindset, you encourage your employees to self-manage. You teach them to deal with problems themselves so that they will not need your help next time. This way, you are making the most of your employees' potential, while stimulating their growth.

1.3   The Mother, the Macho, and the Mole

The theory sounds great, but in practice you will not always manage to stay 'mature,' especially in the face of something that affects or irritates you. Those are precisely the moments you are likely to fall into one of three common pitfalls for managers. In the following, I will describe what it looks like when you walk into one of these pitfalls, what effect it has on your employees, and what beliefs may have created the pitfall in the first place.

The Mother

A well-known leadership pitfall is to slip into the mother role. I call it the mother role, but men and women are both equally likely to walk into this pitfall. It is the tendency to immediately switch to helping and problem-solving mode. This is a reflex of telling an employee how to deal with something, or of comforting an employee or helping an employee put seemingly difficult issues into perspective. What this boils down to is that wanting to help others does not make you a good manager. This is perhaps the most important and hardest part of a coaching leadership style, to let go of the idea that you always have to help.

Employees who are unable to do something or who get stuck will feel powerless and sometimes behave accordingly. You can see it in their faces, or they might even express it verbally: 'Can you help me, I'm lost.' Whenever an employee comes to you with such a request for help or you see the frustration in someone's eyes, your initial reflex will generally be to lend a helping hand. It just feels so natural. When someone says 'help,' you help. Humanity is based on being nice and helpful to others. Without giving it a second thought, you give tips and advice. And you delve right into it, telling your employee, 'Here's what you should do,' or by asking a leading question such as 'Have you tried to ...?'

The Effects of the Mother Role

'What's wrong with good advice?' you might now think, 'What's wrong with the mother role?' First of all, giving advice rarely works. After all, your advice is your take on another person's situation, based on your own frame of reference. If you, for example, have just read a book on assertiveness, you will suddenly see unassertive people everywhere. You perceive the other with yourself as the guideline. So, whenever you think you are helping your employee with advice, your advice might just be way off the mark. Your employee's life differs greatly from yours, as does your employee's background, upbringing, fears and beliefs.

Imagine this: you tell a friend about a problem you have, and she instantly starts to tell you what to do, but you have already tried everything that she suggests. You have been grappling with the problem for some time, so you know much better than your friend what does and what doesn't work. Having this kind of conversation feels tiresome, and it may even irritate you. This is exactly how your employee may feel when you start giving tips and advice off the top of your head. Your employee may start arguing with you, raise objections, or sometimes seem to go along with what you are saying, while meanwhile disengaging internally. 'But my advice is always so good!' I can just hear you say right now. Well, that actually only makes it worse. If your advice is indeed good advice, you are basically stealing your employee's thunder. You are not giving your employee the

opportunity to autonomously find a solution and you are only confirming your employee's sense of incompetence. Your employee's creativity and problem-solving capacity are not challenged. Perhaps your employee actually enjoys not having to think about a solution, which is equally counterproductive, as it makes your employee dependent on your advice. You are then training your employee to think that whenever he or she has a problem, the manager will solve it. As a result, you will be swamped with work and your employee ceases to grow.

The basic effect of the mother role, therefore, is that it breeds passive employees. It will make employees shirk responsibility, in the knowledge that you will be taking that responsibility away anyway. Basically, you will end up making your employees lazier and more passive, which is precisely what you do not want.

Why You Slip Into the Mother Role

- I am important, and my employees need me

The mother role often gives you the rewarding feeling of being needed and doing your duty as a helper. I recognize that from my personal experience. For years, I solved employees' problems for them. Whenever they were unhappy in their jobs, I would rearrange tasks and keep talking to them until things improved (or seemed to have improved). After such talks, where I solved all kinds of problems for them, I always felt extremely useful and fulfilled. Thanks to me, my employees got the help they needed, or so I thought. In actual fact, however, I was only pushing employees into the child role, making them dependent on me. My employees never had to think for themselves, and therefore never learned to think for themselves. They continued to do what they had been doing all along - evade the problem and pass the buck.

Daphne, a participant in one of my training programs, tells us that she has a co-worker (Jason) whom she feels has temper issues, and who once shouted at another co-worker. When this latter co-worker told Daphne about this, she was shocked. How dare he! He had never been this rude to Daphne, so she decided to go talk to him and make it clear that she doesn't tolerate this kind of behavior.

Was that the mature thing to do? No, it was Daphne slipping into the mother role with her co-worker and the macho role with Jason. The mother role prevents her co-worker from building up more resistance, as she only learns that whenever someone crosses a boundary with her, all she needs to do is go to Daphne. This employee is not learning how to effectively handle unacceptable behavior. When Daphne realized this, she realized that despite her good intentions in protecting her co-worker, she was actually depriving her of the opportunity to grow.

Question: What should Daphne have done for a mature response?
Answer: She could have asked how the co-worker experienced the situation and what she would want to do about it. She could have asked, 'Has this happened to you before? What would you want to do about this situation? What would you want or be able to do?' In short, she could have let her handle it herself.

- I want to be liked

Helping someone boosts my likability. Besides, it feels easier to quickly help out employees who are stuck by telling them how you always handle the same situation. As a result, it is not only a desire to be important, but also a desire to be liked that pushes you into the mother role.

In mature mode, on the other hand, you do not automatically help, but you ask questions first. You assess the situation before you decide whether or not you want to help. You ask, for example, why your employee is struggling in this particular situation, or what the various options are. When I give training to managers, the first thing they always say in response to this is, 'But that's not very nice, is it?' Our basic idea is that it is nice to help someone who is stuck by taking over responsibility for the problem. You are then slipping into the mother role and saying, 'I'll write that email for you.'

A possible way to suppress this reflex is to remember that you are then only helping someone in the short term, while stifling their long-term development. So, it may seem nice to hand your employee the solution on a plate or do your employee's work, but it is a short-term solution and actually rather selfish, because you adopt the mother role to feel better about yourself. Personally, I was rather taken aback by this realization, as I had always felt so good in the mother role. I simply wanted to be nice.

- I want to make a difference for others.

Another reason why managers slip into the mother role is that they are very committed to helping their employees in their personal and professional development. When employees stagnate in their development, or are not making progress quickly enough, mother-style managers tend to want to do something about it. They put more effort into it, come up with suggestions on how to grow faster or get a promotion.

Many managers, and that includes me, have at some point pushed employees toward a certain career move, or offered them ready-made development goals to pursue, always with a view to speeding up their development. But what you are then basically telling an employee is, 'What you came up with yourself is not good or not good enough.' You are taking responsibility for career development off their shoulders and putting it onto yours.

One of your employees regularly says that he is ready for a new career move. You want him to make that career move and you have done everything you can to raise his profile across the company. You had him work on an international project, you regularly mention him to the general manager, and you give him the opportunity to attend conferences. However, you are also seeing that he is not seizing these opportunities. He has co-workers take care of presentations, he underachieves on the international project, and he doesn't go to any of the conferences, claiming that he's too busy. It is beginning to irritate you, and you get tired of the whole situation. When this employee came to you complaining about his lack of career opportunities, you slipped into the mother role. But despite your help, he keeps complaining and takes no ownership of his career development. In fact, he even challenges some of your suggestions ('Nobody ever meets anyone interesting at these conferences anyway').

Question: When you want him to take more responsibility, what should you do?
Answer: Confront him respectfully with the fact that although he says he wants to develop, you are not seeing him take any steps in that direction. And that the effect this is having on you (as his manager) is that you are getting irritated. (See also Section 5.2 on Respectful Confrontation.)

When is it actually a good idea to choose the mother role?

Is the mother role always a bad idea? No, it isn't. Sometimes, it is indeed important to take care of employees. Not out of some reflex, but as a conscious choice. When an employee has ended up in a crisis situation, for example, or when an employee is sick or exhausted and momentarily unable to make decisions or has lost grasp of the situation.

I once had an employee who was going through a messy divorce. Despite that, he kept his head down and worked hard to make a deadline. He had stress symptoms and I noticed that others started to go easy on him. After a while, he started to make mistakes and not do his job as well as before. That's when I made the conscious decision to adopt the mother role, telling him to take it easy and that I wanted to discuss with him what he was and wasn't going to do over the coming period.

The Macho Role

A second pitfall for managers is 'the macho.' You may recognize this one from your own experience as well. Macho managers are great at telling it like it is, expressing whatever they see, think, and feel, but not so great at showing empathy. They will say exactly how they feel about employees' behavior, without taking employees' feelings into consideration. Machos have something to say about everything, ranging from how others do their work, how seriously they take their job, or how they are developing.

The Effects of the Macho Role

As soon as you feel a judgment coming on or actually express one, the foundations of the coaching mindset will dissipate. The other will then feel your disapproval and take your response as criticism. When you feel a judgment coming on, your curiosity will instantly disappear, and you become unable to take the other's perspective. All sense of equality will have disappeared from that moment onward, and so the other will cease to feel secure enough to show vulnerability. Your employee will then be less inclined to share the reasons behind certain behavior.

Like the mother role, the macho role pushes the other into a child role (or keeps the other in a child role), simply because you adopt a judgmental superior position, making the other feel small and criticized. This may manifest itself in well-adjusted and obedient behavior, with your employee doing exactly what you tell or ask your employee to do, like an elementary school student who has just been told off by the teacher. Experienced managers will probably recognize it, situations where you feel that your employees follow you unquestioningly, but do not think for themselves. This is often the result of the macho role.

There is also another childlike role that an employee may adopt, the rebel role. Instead of obeying, the rebel resists. I have seen myself do it. When a manager gives me too many instructions and always knows best, I quickly tune out and think, 'So you think you know everything, why don't you do it yourself!'

If your employee has been pushed into child mode - regardless of the kind of child, obedient or rebel - your employee will not take responsibility. The effect of macho leadership is, therefore, that employees get scared or obediently do as you say. They disengage or they rebel. Either way, not the kind of employee you want on your team.

Mark, a participant in my Coaching Leadership course, has an employee, Liam, who is constantly behind in providing figures. He always hides behind excuses and blames others. Liam passes the buck to his co-workers. Mark is uncomfortable with the situation, because it has gotten out of hand. Mark has had it with this situation. In the macho role, he says to Liam, 'Don't keep passing the blame to others, it's so unprofessional. Just take care of it! Cut the excuses!'

Question: When you want him to take more responsibility, what should you do?
Answer: Respectfully confront him with the fact that you have noticed that he has, on several occasions, pointed to others when things hit a snag. And that the effect this is having on you (as his manager) is that you are getting irritated. Next, check whether he recognizes what you are saying and then tell him what you would like to see happen. (See also Section 5.2 on Respectful Confrontation.)

A Macho in Sheep's Clothing

You may now think that the macho role equals being a dominant or unkind manager, or a rather outspoken, perhaps even blunt, manager. But also, beware of the wolf - or the macho in sheep's clothing in this case. No matter how much you sugarcoat your message, when you are being judgmental, you will still have slipped into the macho role. And this will have an effect on your employee. Be aware of phrases such as, 'Yeah, but what still strikes me as odd is ...' and leading questions such as, 'How did you think this project went?' *C'est le ton qui fait la musique.* If you ask these questions out of genuine curiosity, you are not being a macho. But if you think the project did not go well, and there is a ring of criticism to the way you ask the question, your employee will sense that there is a 'right' and a 'wrong'Answer to the question, and not give the 'real'Answer.

Why You Slip Into the Macho Role

The macho role is often triggered by pity or your personal judgment.

- Pity

You find your employee pathetic and you want to protect him or her. Therefore, you give it to your employee straight, telling your employee exactly what you think about the situation. This behavior is comparable to the mother role, albeit now your judgment takes center stage.

Your secretary, Hannah, receives nasty criticism from a close co-worker about how she does her job. When Hannah comes to you (her manager) to talk about this, you get angry. You tell her that she mustn't put up with it. Who does this co-worker think she is! Your anger encapsulates both judgment and pity. You judge the co-worker who displayed unacceptable behavior, but you also judge Hannah, who allowed it to happen. Due to the fact that you are so forthright in expressing your opinion, Hannah feels even smaller than she already did. She even starts to defend the critical co-worker, saying that she didn't mean to be so rude. By getting so angry, you are depriving Hannah of the opportunity to arrive at a conclusion on the situation herself and take ownership.

Question: If you want Hannah to take ownership herself, what should you do?
Answer: The first step is to ask Hannah how she would want to handle the situation. This will give you an idea of what she considers a possible solution. Perhaps she already intended to stand up for herself and talk to her co-worker. Or she may just have come to you to ask if you have previous experience of this kind of situation. If you were to see a pattern (of Hannah letting others walk all over her), you could confront her with it openly and honestly (also see Section 5.2 on Respectful Confrontation).

• Your Personal Judgment

Sometimes you feel that employees are making the wrong choices, choices that go against your beliefs and values. When, for example, your personal belief is that taking your job seriously means working full-time, you find it hard to accept when one of your employees opts to work four days a week to have one day a week to do other things. Or when you believe that everyone must try to get ahead in their careers, you will clash with employees who are content in their current roles and feel no need to move up in the company. You are judging employees' behavior, work ethic, home life, or the work they do based on your own personal beliefs.

The question is how to put aside those beliefs. This is not easy. But it is not impossible either. It will help if you become mindful of your beliefs, of your tendency to judge, and of the fact that your judging makes your employee feel smaller. The way to be less judgmental is to 'turn on' your curiosity. Take your employee's perspective, try to imagine how things are for your employee. Ask yourself what it is like to be your employee and to feel like your employee. If you then realize that your employee's behavior really triggers a resistance overload in you and you are unable to be genuinely interested in your employee, it is best to not have that talk just yet. It would then be better to engage in some introspection and figure out if you want to take it further. You could, for example, talk to someone (a coach) to explore why you are so judgmental toward this employee and what you can do to still have an engaging and constructive working relationship with this employee.

During a training course, one of the managers, Gemma, tells me that her employee Charles is driving her to despair. He doesn't meet commitments, seems to completely ignore things they agreed on, and he takes ages to respond to emails or doesn't respond at all. Gemma is slowly getting more and more frustrated by his neglectful behavior. She starts to monitor him more closely and becomes increasingly insistent in asking him what he is doing. And yet, she's not seeing any improvement. In fact, he seems to be sharing even less with Gemma.

Question: If you, as the manager, want Charles to take more responsibility, what should you do?

Answer: Be open and honest about what you have seen happen. Tell him what effect it is having on you, and what you would like to see change. When Gemma engaged in this kind of frank conversation with Charles and told him what she had seen, Charles explained that he is very worried about his brother. He didn't want to let on that he had something on his

> mind. He tried to hide his concern behind a nonchalant attitude. He actually tried to keep Gemma at a distance, because her insistent tone started to irritate him.

When is it actually a good idea to choose the macho role?

- Wake up

Sometimes, it is important to just wake an employee up by telling him or her directly and in no uncertain terms how certain behavior comes across. Or to confront someone with the fact that they are not making progress. This does not mean you are acting out of impatience, judgmentalism, or irritation, but rather out of a conscious choice to take this approach and because you are helping your employee get ahead.

- Fire

There are situations where the macho role is really the only appropriate role. One example is in case of a fire. If there is literally a fire in the building, you are not going to sit down with your colleagues to discuss how they think the fire should be handled. Quite the opposite, you give orders and make sure everyone does exactly what you say. It can, of course, also be a proverbial fire, a presentation that needs to be on the board's desk within an hour or a serious complaint that must be dealt with right away. Therefore, you can consciously choose to deploy the macho role, which means that you choose to address employees based on your (better) judgment. However, if you end up doing that quite often, you sure have a lot of fires to put out. If that is indeed the case, it would be wise to talk to your employees about how to prevent those fires in the first place.

Macho Professions

There are professions where you, as the manager, will often be in macho mode, simply because the profession involves giving strict orders that need to be carried out. Examples include a surgeon or movie director who delivers a steady stream of commands to others. Not until after the surgery or shoot is there an opportunity for everyone to discuss. Then, too, the effect of the macho role is that your employees are in child mode, obediently doing what you tell them to and taking little responsibility themselves. But that is what is supposed to happen in those situations. It is perfectly fine to deliberately choose to use a specific role because you feel it is necessary. The thing is not to slip into a role by accident or unwittingly, because that is when it is a reflex. It is good to be mindful of your reflexes and their effects, as that will empower you to take control of your actions and consciously choose a style to match the situation.

The Mole Role

A mole is a manager who lacks courage or who has given up, who has simply ceased to enter into conversation. This is a manager with a disengaged 'whatever' mindset. Moles know there are issues that need to be addressed, but they choose not to. Moles withdraw into their molehill and stay in their comfort zone. This is because they are afraid, insecure, or have tuned out.

- You have an employee who is often late, but you let it go because he does a good job.
- One employee tends to wear rather revealing outfits and overdoes it on the make-up. You know that she wants to come across as more serious, but you are afraid to tell her that her appearance is partly why she is not taken seriously.
- Your employee is often blunt and curt in interactions with his co-workers. You know that his co-workers gossip about him behind his back. But when you go to talk to him about it, you think that he may take you for a bit of a softie, so you say nothing.
- Your employee is very good at what she does, but she is such a perfectionist that it takes her a lot more time to complete tasks than her co-workers. You do not want to dishearten her, so you choose not to tell her.
- One of your employees shows little initiative. You have already raised this issue with him several times and you are tired of it, so you think, 'Never mind, there's no point in bringing it up now.'

The Effects of the Mole Role

If you do not speak up, you are not taking responsibility. The effect on your employee is that his or her behavior does not improve. You hope your employee will realize it and change of his or her own accord, but this seldom happens. Chances are, in fact, that your employee's behavior will only get worse, as your employee is oblivious to the error of his or her ways.

Why You Slip Into the Mole Role

- You are afraid or insecure

You are plagued by anxiety whenever you intend to address something. Out of a sense of fear, you choose to let sleeping dogs lie and not confront anyone with their attitude or behavior. You are unsure as to whether it is your place to say what you have to say.

Many managers are afraid that being straight with people about things that are not going well will reduce their likability. Or they are afraid that it will make employees less motivated.

I once had an employee who was often very critical of the company's management and how things were organized. She also believed that there was a lack of capacity and budget for her particular domain. She complained about this quite a lot. When I suggested to her that she could put in a request for more staff, and make a case for it by proving it would bring in more business (on a side note: can you see that I slipped into the mother role here? I tried to solve her problem for her), she was not keen on the idea. She said, 'That'll never be accepted.'

When she complained again later, I snapped and told her that she should just put together a proposal offsetting the costs of an extra employee against the greater revenue (hello macho role!). Two weeks later, I received a Word document with a ten-line proposal without any real reasoning behind it. I instantly knew that it would never get us the extra capacity she wanted. I wasn't sure whether to ask her to redo the proposal. But I was also afraid to crush her spirit and have her complaining to me about how complicated such a request for capacity is, so I made the proposal myself.

So, there you have it, I switched from mother role to macho role and back to mother role. But I also slipped into the mole role at one point. I thought she was not putting in the required effort. And I also thought that she put the work on my plate as a result. And I felt that all she was doing was complain, instead of actually taking action. But I didn't tell her any of this. That's what I call 'moling.' You see what's happening, but you don't say anything about it.

- You disengage

If an employee still fails to take action after a few talks, you may develop a tendency to just say 'whatever' and let it go. Nothing seems to work with this person. Nothing you do seems to have any effect. At one point, you simply lose the will and energy to confront the employee. Besides, you will have run out of pointers to give to your employee, so you just let it go.

In some cases, this is due to the fact that you already have a negative opinion of the other. But it could also be that you have tried to do too much, that you were in mother mode.

When is it actually a good idea to choose the mole role?

Sometimes it makes sense to stand back and not intervene, simply because you do not know exactly what is going on. Being a mole can actually serve a purpose in some cases, such as when you are trying to identify a pattern. Or when you are exploring what it is exactly that irritates you so much or what you keep coming up against with your employees. This is when mole mode is not a reflex, but a choice, a choice to delay having your say until you have a better grasp of the situation.

You can also choose to stay in mole mode when it is simply not the time or place to say what you think or feel. In a packed meeting room or when someone is extremely stressed, it may be better to wait until you are alone with your employee or until your employee is open to your feedback. Choosing the right time can be tricky, because these circumstances are often also used as excuses to get out of saying anything at all.

A while back, I partnered with an actor in a training session on how to give feedback. The session was in English and he struggled to get his message across because of the language barrier. As a result, I had to pull out all the stops and do most of the work myself, which I found rather irritating. When I told a co-worker about this, she asked if I had said anything about this to the actor. I said I hadn't, because I had to leave immediately after the session and there was also another trainer in the room. I therefore had a good reason not to engage with the actor on this issue.

Or was it an excuse? I could have called him. But I thought, 'Hmm, who am I to take issue with his acting skills?' He was working for us on a freelance basis, so I would just request a different actor next time, so that I wouldn't have to hurt his feelings. And that was another excuse.

In the end, I called him and told him how I had felt during the session. My words startled him, but he was ultimately very understanding. And I felt a lot better about the whole thing. Also because I will definitely be asking him for Dutch-language jobs in the future. If I hadn't said anything, I would have kept avoiding him.

I am using this example to illustrate that it can be a conscious choice to delay confronting someone with their behavior or attitude.

But do always be honest with yourself. Is it really a choice? Or is it an excuse to get out of having a difficult conversation, as was the case for me here?

Switching Roles

It is not that you ARE a mother manager or a macho manager. It is just that you occasionally slip into these roles. Most managers will be aware of all the pitfalls. And even within one conversation, you can inadvertently switch from mole mode to mother mode to macho mode within a time span of only a few minutes. Certain role changes are more common than others.

If you keep your mouth shut about something that bothers you, your level of irritation will gradually go up as these annoying occurrences keep happening. This is what I refer to as 'drawing straws.' Imagine your employee does something that annoys you, but you do not say anything about it. In your head, however, you do keep a tally of all these irritations, these straws. Whenever your employee does something wrong, you draw another straw. Nobody knows that these straws are accumulating in your head. In fact, you may not even realize you are doing it.

Then, one day, you reach your limit, you draw the straw that breaks the camel's back. And that is when you get angry and just blurt it out, without any kind of tact. You had been in mole mode for too long. And now you suddenly slip into the macho role.

Celine, a participant in one of my leadership programs, tells the group that her co-worker Jonathan often comes in late for work. He comes in at 9.30am and when she gives him a surprised look, he says, with a big smile on his face, 'On the dot, right?' It kept happening, even though Celine had made it clear that she thought it was unacceptable. So, one day, Celine couldn't take it any longer and told him that this behavior really wasn't normal, that he should come in on time, take his job seriously, and have the decency not to saddle his co-workers with the preparations for a presentation he is supposed to give. And she also told him that if he comes in late again, she will take him off this account.

Due to the fact Celine had been stuck in mole mode for a while, thinking a disapproving look would be enough to make him see the error of his ways, she suddenly slipped into the macho role and told him off.

Question: What would have been a mature response?
Answer: To respectfully confront Jonathan with his unacceptable behavior, and, from a position of equals, let him know what is happening between them and what effect this is having on her (see also Section 5.2 on Respectful Confrontation).

I think everyone will recognize this situation. And it is not even a bad thing to get angry with someone who is slacking off. But if you have kept your mouth shut for too long, you will suddenly slip into the macho role and become very judgmental and resort to punishment. This kind of outburst pushes the employee into the child role. Your employee will then generally only be preoccupied with defending himself or herself, and ultimately not take responsibility. At best, your employee will briefly do as you demanded, out of fear.

From Mother Mode to Macho Mode

Whenever you have been in mother mode for a prolonged period of time, giving lots of advice, perhaps even helping your employee get started, and you notice that your employee is not acting on your advice, the resulting irritation may push you into macho mode. You get angry and become judgmental. And your employee can hear that in your voice. You are not giving pure feedback, but your feedback is colored by your judgment.

> Imagine you have an employee who is very stressed, and you have spoken to him about it on several occasions. He tells you he would like to go home earlier every day so that he can do more relaxing things at home. But time and time again, he fails to do so. You even emailed him an mp3 with mindfulness exercises, but he hasn't even listened to it. You say to him, 'This is not working with you, because you don't do what you say you're going to do anyway.' Now you're in macho mode. You communicate like a macho. You are not calmly sharing your observations. You have lost your curiosity.

From Mother or Macho to Mole

If you have been in mother or macho mode for a while, you will ultimately get tired of it. This is because it is hard work to keep coming up with solutions and giving advice. And so, you may switch from mother to macho mode, or perhaps even directly from mother or macho to mole mode. Mentally drained, you think, 'Whatever.' Whatever I do, we are not getting anywhere. And then you disengage and stop investing your time in your employee. You do not say what you feel, or you duck the issue altogether.

> I once had an employee who was very chaotic. He worked very hard, but his head was always all over the place. Nobody knew what he was working on, which made his environment - and that included me - restless. I did all kinds of things for him to help him get organized. I made to-do lists for him, got him a coach, enrolled him in a time management course (a very motherly thing to do, I know), but none of it worked.
> After some time, it had worn me out completely. So much so, in fact, that I tuned out and stopped addressing his disorderliness. But I didn't tell him that it was still bothering me and that it was thwarting his development (mole).

- Is there a particular employee who often makes you slip into the mother role? What does this person do to push you into mother mode?
- Which conversations do you avoid? Who would hear the truth if you were to stop being a mole?
- And who often triggers a macho response from you? What does this person do to push you into macho mode?
- Is there anyone who stays in mother or macho mode toward you?

1.4   Dealing with Needs for Help

As I described earlier, when you have been in mother mode for a while, you will often get tired of it and get irritated. If you have put in considerable effort in trying to help someone and it seems not to have had any effect or your employee is simply not taking it in, chances are that you will start criticizing your employee. This is when you enter the drama triangle.

The drama triangle (see Figure 1.2) (as also used in Transactional Analysis) shows how easily (and often) you get caught up in a certain pattern. Luckily, the model also shows how to break out of it. But what is better still is to prevent ending up in the drama triangle altogether. The drama triangle is a kind of role play that people engage in without realizing it. It is interaction based on inequality, where each role feels superior or inferior to the other. And nobody takes responsibility. Sounds bad, doesn't it?

The three roles in the drama triangle are that of victim, rescuer, and persecutor. And these roles keep switching between the different persons in the triangle. If you look closely, you may recognize the mother and the macho in these roles.

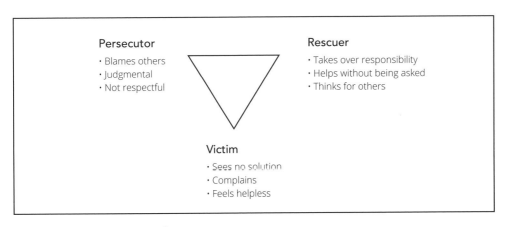

Persecutor
· Blames others
· Judgmental
· Not respectful

Rescuer
· Takes over responsibility
· Helps without being asked
· Thinks for others

Victim
· Sees no solution
· Complains
· Feels helpless

Figure 1.2   The Drama Triangle

The Victim

The victim is a complainer, someone who adopts the attitude of a helpless child. In real life, the victim is a moaner, a grouch, an employee who is (temporarily) stuck. But a victim is also someone who you think could do better. An employee who, in your opinion, could grow faster or could perform better.

> Diana complains to her manager, Jacob, that she is unable to do her job properly because her co-workers are continuously late in delivering the copy she needs. There is nothing she can do about it, so she says, and she's already tried everything. She keeps going on about how she's unable to work this way!

The Rescuer

The rescuer wants to rescue the victim and, therefore, gives (unsolicited) advice, thinks for the other, and takes over responsibility (just like a manager in mother mode does). In the beginning, rescuers often enjoy their role, as they feel important and useful. Just like me. I always felt very valuable when I was able to help my co-workers solve problems. But rescuers forget to stand up for their own needs and therefore ultimately waste a lot of energy.

> Back to the real-life example of Diana and Jacob. Jacob has asked the communications manager on several occasions to make sure his department delivers the copy on time. He has also explained to Diana that she should get her co-workers involved in the process at an earlier stage. And that she should communicate more firmly in her emails. In other words, Jacob is trying to solve Diana's problems for her, without her ever asking him to.

The Persecutor

The persecutor judges and accuses the other. Persecutors do not think and speak respectfully about the other. They are angry or annoyed and blame it on the other (macho).

> Jacob gets irritated. He sees that Diana, despite his help and good advice, does not change. She just moans, in his view, without taking any action herself. He simply cannot stand it anymore, all her complaining, because he feels she should've acted on his advice.

In the drama triangle, you switch roles without realizing it. The drama triangle generally kicks off when a rescuer starts to help someone (the victim), often unsolicited, because they take pity on this person, because they think they can do or know better, or because they get impatient. Rescuer and victim keep this interaction up for a while, until either (or even both) switches to the persecutor role.

As soon as it becomes clear that the victim does not do what the rescuer wants, the rescuer is likely to turn into a persecutor and start to accuse and judge the victim. What an annoying victim, he doesn't listen! The victim is then pushed even deeper into the victim role, or also switches to the persecutor role, incensed at the treatment by the other (who used to be the rescuer). Or the victim turns into the rescuer and tries to make it up with the other by rescuing the other. The one who started out as the rescuer may also, via the persecutor role, switch to the victim role: 'Can nobody see what I've done for him?'

Are you still with me? A role-play situation where you switch roles. You can go from victim to persecutor, but also from rescuer to persecutor.

> Your employee complains about her workload and tells you that she is having trouble sleeping. You want to help her. You take some work off her plate, give her an extra day off, and send her an interesting article about job pressure and stress. In other words, you're in rescuer mode.
>
> Two weeks later, it turns out that she has not taken that day off yet and hasn't read the article either. She claims she was too busy. Internally, you are now starting to judge her, finding her ungrateful. And perhaps you even externalize your irritation by saying, 'How do you expect to get fit if you won't address your sleeping problems?' Instead of showing an interest in her, you get angry with her. She feels judged and becomes even more pitiful, even more of a victim. 'Listen, I just can't do it, it's all too much for me,' she says. Or she also morphs into a persecutor, saying, 'Those articles you sent me were useless.' Or she enters rescuer mode and says, 'You're right, it was my fault that it didn't work.'

From Drama to Winners
But how do you break out of this triangle, out of the drama? The drama triangle can become a winners triangle if we recalibrate the three positions.
- A rescuer can become a *helper* by striking a balance between giving and taking, between looking out for number one and taking care of others. As a manager, you may sometimes find that you want to 'rescue' an employee who is truly stuck. If you, instead of automatically starting to rescue, consciously choose to offer help, rescuing turns into 'helping.' This also means that you do not provide unsolicited help, but instead ask how you can help.

> Personally, I tend to try to introduce anyone who's looking for a job to interesting people from my network, but people do not always want that kind of help. Now, before I try to refer someone, I ask, 'Would you like me to introduce you to a few people?' This allows the other to let me know whether or not it would indeed be helpful to them.

- A victim can learn to be realistic. This means being honest about how you feel and asking for help when you are stuck. You will then not be a victim, but instead a realist in the winners triangle. Asking for help is not the same as being a victim. A victim pretends not to be able to do something or not to know something, faking helplessness. A realist basically says, 'I can do all kinds of things, but I have just briefly got stuck.' And this is actually very mature. It is even very helpful when your employee is clear about what he or she wants from you as a manager.

> My co-workers used to come to me quite often with questions about a complaint that had come in, for example, or a difficult question from a customer. When I first heard about the drama triangle, I realized my employees were somewhat victimlike toward me when they came to me with a problem. And that I never even hesitated to take on the rescuer role.
>
> So, I asked them to first think about a possible solution themselves, and that I would prefer it if they came to me with a proposal instead of a question. This way, I intended to keep them out of the victim role and turn them into employees who are aware of their capabilities and who only ask for help when they really need it. After that, I became better at not immediately wanting to come to the rescue. And this, in turn, gave my employees greater confidence and saved me a lot of energy.

- If you do not want to stay in the persecutor role, you need to be more assertive. Be clear about what your boundaries are and speak up about anything you do not like. Communicate what you have seen the other do, what effect it has on you, and what you would want the other to do. This is a simple way to prevent getting irritated and becoming a persecutor.

> - Describe a drama triangle that you are currently in.
> - What step can you take to get out of this drama triangle?
> - Are any of your employees in a drama triangle with each other or with others? What could they do differently?

1.5   Summary

Mature leadership is managing with the mindset that your employees are responsible for their own tasks, job satisfaction, and health, based on a belief that they are capable of taking care of themselves.

When everything is running smoothly, being a mature (or coaching) manager is easy, but as soon as things cease to go your way, the pitfalls appear.

One pitfall is you slipping into the mother role, as you want to rescue your employee, solve your employee's problem, because you think that is you being nice, or because you think your employee simply cannot manage without your help. However, this will only make your employee lazy. A second pitfall is the macho role, which is when you start telling your employee what to do, or when you turn your irritation into a judgment. Again, it will make your employee more passive, and perhaps even somewhat afraid. Your employee may also go to the other extreme and adapt to you too much. The third pitfall is mole mode, which is when you choose not to address what you really should be addressing. Out of fear or because you just do not feel like it.

Even in difficult situations, there is a way to be mature in your responses. That is what this book is all about. If you manage from a mature mindset, you are establishing equality in your interaction and not taking responsibility away from employees, not even when an employee appears to be helpless.

With the pitfalls identified, the next chapter will go into the various leadership skills that are essential for managers.

2 Leadership Skills

In leadership, there are several skills that you cannot do without. It will come in handy if you have the ability to switch between different leadership styles, tailoring your approach to your employees' needs at any given moment. If you want your employees to take on more responsibility, it is key that you know how to assume the responsibility that goes with your role. This means, among other things, that you keep an eye on the bigger picture and make strategic choices that contribute to your company's success. Aside from that, you need conversation skills, which will also be addressed in this chapter, showing you how to control conversations.

2.1   Situational Leadership

As I described in Section 1.3 in reference to the mother, macho, and mole pitfalls, you can actually make a conscious choice to use these roles to achieve a specific effect. You could, for example, choose to adopt the mother role momentarily to support an overworked employee, or behave like a macho to get your team to shift up a gear for a specific task. Many managers take their own preferences as their frame of reference, managing in the way they like to be managed. But this is not always the way your employees like or need to be managed. This chapter is about what your employees need. How to choose leadership styles and tailor these styles to what your employees need will be set out clearly using the situational leadership model. This model (developed by Hersey and Blanchard (2007)) says that every employee needs a different leadership style from their manager based on the task at hand. It also shows where things go wrong sometimes when you, as a manager, try to give your employees responsibility and adopt a coaching-based leadership style. Meanwhile, several different variations on this theory have emerged as the people behind it have each gone their separate ways and continued to develop the model in different directions.

Personally, I prefer the clarity of the version shown in Figure 2.1. The basis of the situational leadership philosophy is that there are four leadership styles, ranging from high task focus and high relationship focus to a combination of both and no task and relationship focus at all. Hersey and Blanchard show that the ideal style is the one that is best aligned with what your employee needs to grow in terms of the performance of his or her task. The indicator they created for this is *task maturity*, which specifies how able and willing an employee is to perform a certain task. The style you choose depends on the employee's level of experience performing the task and your employee's level of self-confidence. Choosing the right style will enable you, as the manager, to help your employee grow.

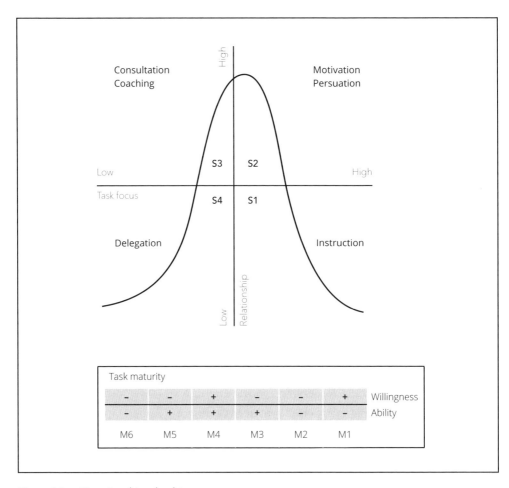

Figure 2.1   Situational Leadership

To be able to adapt your style, you first need to know your employee's level of task maturity, meaning how 'able' and 'willing' your employee is. By 'able' the model means your employee's level of knowledge and competence, the skills your employee possesses. Has your employee had enough guidance, training, and time to gain experience? Ability is not always apparent from behavior. If your employee performs poorly, this may also be due to a lack of motivation or self-confidence. This is what the model refers to as willingness. When an employee simply does not see the point of a certain task, or suffers from stress or other problems, performance may be affected considerably.

Every stage of task maturity (M) goes with a leadership style.

Instruction

When you look at the table at the bottom of Figure 2.1, you can see that employees who are assigned a new task start out in M1. They are not very competent yet in certain areas (due to their lack of experience), but they are willing and motivated. This is when you go for the instruction-based leadership style (S1), telling your employee (in great detail, if necessary) how the task is done, what you expect from your employee, and what the relevant procedures are. Lots of directing, little support. This is a task-driven style. The pitfall that looms is that you become overly instructional (macho) or stay in this mode for too long.

Motivation/Persuasion

When your employee has been doing the task for longer, your employee's task maturity will increase, and your employee will move into M2. This is the point of low ability and low willingness. The employee realizes that there are many things that he or she does not know (yet) or your employee is not yet fully committed to and excited about the task. The leadership style to match this stage is the one of motivation and persuasion (S2). With your approach as the basis, you tell your employee why you want things done a certain way. At the same time, you do a lot of directing and supporting. You continue to give instructions, but you also work on your employee's attitude, adopting a focus on both the task and the relationship. The pitfall is that you help too much or simply take over (mother mode).

Consultation, Coaching

Once your employee has been performing the task for some time, your employee will know how it is done (high ability), but will not always feel like doing it, or perhaps be insecure sometimes (low willingness). Your employee knows what to do but hesitates or has doubts. Or your employee does not agree with the assignment or approach.

The style you need to adopt for M3 is S3, meaning that you need to consult and coach. Instructions are no longer needed, but instead you give your employee responsibility by asking questions. You could ask your employee, 'What causes you to be anxious about this task?' Talk to your employee about things that are tricky and coach your employee as and when necessary. Your focus is not on the task, but on the person. The pitfall here is that you overpsychologize things or start asking questions when you actually want to tell your employee something (mole mode).

Delegation

For many managers, the last of the four quadrants (bottom left) is the holy grail. Your employee is both willing and able to perform a certain task (M4). Your employee is task mature! You can leave the task to your employee. This style is called delegation. You do not give instructions, and you give little to no support. This leadership style is not focused on the task, but not on the relationship either. A possible pitfall here is that you make your employee completely responsible for the task, as well as for other things, and no longer discuss them (mole mode). Or that what you are doing is not actually delegating but neglecting (such as when you mistakenly believe that your employee is ready for it). It is, therefore, important that you still keep liaising with your employee when delegating tasks.

The Risk of M5 and M6

Most managers find delegation less strenuous than instruction or coaching. But when your employee has graduated to M4 for a number of tasks, another risk arises, as shown in the table at the bottom of Figure 2.1. When you get to the point where your employee performs tasks autonomously, boredom looms. Your employee has got the task down to a tee, but motivation levels start to dwindle. This is when the 'been there, done that' mindset takes root. And if this employee is someone with a lot of influence internally, his or her negative attitude may rub off on the rest of the team.

In that case, the thing to do as the manager is to engage with your employee, confront your employee respectfully with his or her performance, exploring together what your employee needs to experience more of a challenge.

If your employee has been in M5 for a while, your employee may drop back to M6. This happens when your employee has not felt committed and motivated for so long that it has an adverse effect on his or her ability. This happens to employees who struggle to keep up with (technological) developments. You should then avoid mole mode (leaving your employee to it or not paying any attention to your employee), and instead engage with your employee.

Situational leadership is all about observing your employees well and adapting your style based on your assessment of each employee's task maturity for each specific task. But beware, you cannot pigeon-hole your employees. You cannot simply say that 'Mary is in M2' because although she is very good at sending emails without help, she may still struggle with other tasks such as calling customers. You must assess task maturity for each task separately. Still, you could say about Mary that 'she is in M4 when it comes to sending mailings and she is in M2 when it comes to calling customers.'

Step by Step

Situational leadership makes you think in terms of steps, steps from S1 to S2 and only then to S3. And in the opposite direction as well. When things go wrong, for example when your employee is in M4 and makes a mistake, you must also downshift to the preceding leadership style and start coaching and consulting again (S3). You discuss what happened and ask why it happened. Many managers (and I also recognize this from my own experience) are so shocked when an employee to whom they delegated tasks underachieves that they instantly revert to the instruction-based style (S1). But remember, your employee already knows how to do it! Your employee knows what to do, but something happened, that's all. Instructions on how to perform the task are not helpful in this kind of situation, so your response is way off the mark. Instead, you need to find out what happened.

> Training participant Sean shared the following case. He had put his employee Florence in charge of organizing an event. She had extensive experience with this specific task, so he delegated the whole process of sending out invitations to her (S4). Five weeks before the event, Sean noticed that the invitations hadn't been sent out yet. Upset, he told Florence that everyone really needed to have an invitation in their inbox in time for the event. He told her where she could find the address details and how to send the email. In other words, Sean went from delegation (S4) back to instruction (S1). But what he should have done is take a step back first and ask Florence why the invitations hadn't been sent yet. He could then have discussed the reasons behind her approach with her. Or, if it turned out that she needed help, he could've coached her in planning these kinds of things.

How to Assess Your Employee's Task Maturity

In some cases, it may not be instantly clear how task mature your employee is. If so, you can always just ask. If your employee repeatedly fails to send out a mailing on time, you can ask, 'How come you haven't sent the mailing yet?' and 'Would it help if

I were to explain the procedure again or is there anything else wrong?' By letting the employee decide, you prevent that you start doing something that will in no way help your employaee (and it also prevents mother or macho behavior).

In Closing

The situational leadership model is particularly relevant, in my view, because it shows how to get the most out your employees. By aligning your style with your employees' level of task maturity, you become able to help them progress, which will make them grow and allow them to gradually take more responsibility. And that is when they will lighten your workload. Sometimes, it may even be expedient to take an even more detailed look at a task and adapt your style accordingly.

> A manager in one of my training sessions, Rose, told the group that she has an employee who is good at customer contact. He makes eye contact, is good at presenting selling points, and he actually gets deals done. But when dealing with a slightly older, more senior customer, he is unable to take on this sparring partner role, as he would then be overly jovial toward them. Rose did sense that her employee wouldn't be helped by instructions on how to handle sales talks. After all, he knows very well how to sell, so he would instantly tune out. As far as selling is concerned, he is in M3 or even M4. But where he could do with some additional instruction is on how to introduce a greater level of equality into sales talks when dealing with an older and more distinguished customer. Or, perhaps he does know how to handle these kinds of customers but is afraid to present himself as an equal. The only way to find out is by talking to him about it.

Another handy piece of guidance from situational leadership is that your leadership style should always keep you one step ahead of your employee. If you think your employee is ready for the next step, preempt it by already moving on to the style for the next quadrant. This way, you are basically towing your employee through the stages.

An employee who is reasonably task mature and regularly performs the task without problems, but who is somewhat insecure at times, would benefit from coaching (S3) during the task. After a while, you can also start delegating (S4). You will then basically push your employee into the next quadrant through the leadership style you adopt.

- You probably have a preferred leadership style. What is it? And for which tasks for which employees is that not the ideal style to adopt?
- Does your company, as a whole, have a preferred style, a leadership style that is used and appreciated in the higher echelons of your company?
- Think of two of your employees, preferably a highly experienced one and a relatively new one. What are their main tasks and where are they in terms of task maturity and willingness? Do you offer them the right support?

2.2   Taking Ownership

Mature leadership also means taking ownership. That said, sometimes things do not go the way you want them to go. Perhaps you are annoyed by underachieving employees. Or perhaps your manager never has time for you. Or perhaps the way the IT department works causes you problems. The Control Model (Figure 2.2) can help you feel better when things are not going your way, when things are not going as well as you had hoped.

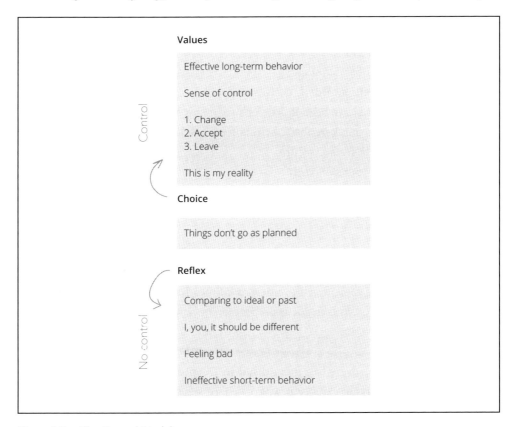

Figure 2.2   The Control Model

The Control Model shows how you, as a manager, can take ownership, even when things are not going your way. In such situations, you can start complaining and rebelling, but that will generally not make you feel any better. What will make you feel better is if you take ownership of the situation. You always have a choice. You can change the situation, accept it, or leave. Choosing any of these three options, and behaving accordingly, will give you a sense of control. On top of that, it will ensure that you stay true to your values.

When Things Don't Go As Expected/Planned

Sometimes, things do not go as you had planned. Co-workers are not up to your expectations or your own performance is not up to your expectations. This happens when you, for example, are looking forward to getting home at the end of the day and end up in traffic on your way home, or when you expected to deliver a smooth self-confident presentation but turned out to be nervous after all, or when your manager did not give you the compliment you expected. Many of these situations, perhaps even as many as one hundred a day, are easy to accept by just putting up with them and moving on. But sometimes you find yourself unable to just put up with it. It keeps playing in your mind or it bothers you.

There are three kinds of situations that can make you insecure or angry, and make you feel that you are not in control.

1. *You are not up to your own standards*
   Example: After a meeting, Aidan receives feedback from a co-worker. The co-worker tells him that he could have been less defensive in how he responded to the questions he was asked. Aidan is taken aback by this feedback and worries that he may have come across badly. He feels insecure.

2. *The other is not up to your standards.*
   Example: Georgia is angry. Her co-workers have, without her knowing and without discussing it first, rescheduled an MT meeting to a time when Georgia cannot attend. She feels passed over.

3. *The situation is not up to your standards.*
   Example: Peter is unable to accept the changes that are happening at the company where he works. He feels that the internal culture has become too cut-throat. He would like there to be a greater focus on people, the way it used to be. He is annoyed.

Reflexes

Reflexes (which will be covered in great detail in Chapter 7) are mental, sensory, and behavioral automatisms that can occur when we face sensitive issues. These issues are, as it were, a kind of bruising on our soul. When such a bruise is touched, a reflex is triggered that basically repeats the behavior we have always had in response to the issue in question. The control model in the previous section has these reflexes in the bottom of the model, denoting the behavioral patterns that we relapse into time and time again.

Whenever a situation deviates from how you expected it be, you instantly start comparing and judging. You compare the situation to something that happened in the past or to your ideal. You may, for example, expect employees to take their work seriously and always work hard, basically applying your ideal to your employees. But we also create ideals for our own performance. You may, for example, find it very important to always respond with quick wit. Whenever you do not comply with your own ideal, it bothers you.

- Aidan, who was just told he went on the defensive too much and could have responded in a more open fashion, would have liked to have shared an image of himself as someone who is open to feedback. This was his ideal.
- The ideal that Georgia, who is angry with her co-workers, has in mind is that everyone takes her into consideration.
- Peter, who is frustrated with the corporate culture at his company, has an ideal image of his company as one with more human qualities.

Losing Control

When you get frustrated because others, the situation, or you yourself fail to comply with your ideal, you are effectively relinquishing control of how you feel. You are basically telling yourself that things should not be the way they are, which leads you to judge others, the situation, or yourself.

So, now the situation determines how you feel. The fact that you did not get the compliment you expected makes you feel upset. The fact that a meeting was rescheduled behind your back makes you feel angry. Your company becoming a harsher work environment makes you feel disappointed. You have become the victim of your own ideal. As psychologists typically say, 'Your unhappiness is not caused by the situation, but by your thoughts about it.'

And what do you do when you feel frustrated? You start to complain, gossip, eat, disengage, scream, etc. You fall back on your reflexes, behavior you have used in similar situations in the past. But these reflexes do not change the situation. In fact, they only reinforce the situation.

- Aidan, who felt insecure due to the feedback, stayed home sick the next day, even though he was committed to his project.
- Georgia started to ignore her fellow MT members, which led to them taking even less notice of her.
- Peter started to complain a lot and co-workers began avoiding him as a result, making his work environment even harsher.

Sometimes, these kinds of short-term responses briefly make you feel better (often like a sense of relief), but they do not lead to any improvement in the long term. This brief mood swing happens because we do not have to feel our unpleasant feelings for a little while. And these short-term responses are often incompatible with our values, with what we find important and the image of ourselves we want to get across. Just imagine what you do when you feel frustrated. Is that who you want to be, how you want to be perceived?

Looking at the examples of Aidan, Georgia, and Peter, we can see that their behavior (staying home sick, ignoring others, and moaning) is not in keeping with their values. It is not compatible with the way they want to come across as a person or a leader.

How to Regain Control

And now for the good news: anyone can break out of this downward spiral at any time and return to an upward trajectory. Again, I will start at the same point, at the center of Figure 2.2: *Things don't go as planned*. But now we move upward, to choice instead of reflex, to taking control.

Whenever something does not go as you had expected or planned, choose not to lapse into a reflex. Adopt a mature attitude. Instead of making yourself the victim of the situation (small), respond in a mature manner. Do not compare the disappointing situation to the past or to your ideal but look only at the facts. And the facts are 'I didn't get a compliment' and 'I responded awkwardly to questions after my presentation.' Do not blow facts out of proportion and do not go against reality by thinking, 'This is not how it's supposed to go!'

The reality you accept is, for example, 'I have one of those managers who doesn't do compliments.' It does not mean, however, that you have to enjoy this reality, it is okay to have negative feelings about it. Reality can make you angry or afraid. It is a feeling that simply goes with the situation. But what you are not doing now is fighting a futile fight against reality and thinking that things should not be this way.

Reality is what it is, and you accept that. In Aidan's example, reality is that he was not able to show in his presentation what he wanted to show. That was unfortunate, but there is nothing he can do about it now. As soon as his mindset switches to 'Okay, this is my reality,' he can take ownership and move into the top half of the Control Model. Georgia, too, can accept reality, as in 'This is my situation, the meeting was rescheduled without me.' And Peter could think, 'It is what it is, the company has become less considerate than it used to be. I don't like it, but it's just the way it is.'

Change, Accept, Leave!

If you manage to stop fighting the situation, you will already have made the first step. The next step to take to feel more in control is to choose one of three options: change, accept, or leave.

1. The first question you can ask yourself at this point is, 'Can I change the situation?' If you can, do it! So, if you are frustrated by something your manager does and you have not spoken to him or her about it, go and talk about it.

2. If your response is, 'No, I'm afraid to' or 'I've tried that already,' the next question to ask yourself is, 'Can I accept it?' If theAnswer is 'yes,' accept it and move on. Accept your manager for who he or she is and stop fighting it. Focus on things you do have control over.

3. If you cannot accept the situation or continue to moan about it, the next logical step is to leave. Perhaps leaving is what you should do, exiting the situation that is causing you so much frustration, and resigning, for example. Sometimes, you cannot just resign, or the situation is not serious enough for you to resign over. If this is the case, start at the top again, 'Can you change it?'

If one of the three options is not an option for you, there are only two remaining options. And in some cases, there is only one option. Therefore, if changing is impossible (such as when you are stuck in traffic on your way home from work), you can still choose between accepting it and leaving. However, since leaving is not an option either when you are stuck in traffic, your only option is to just accept it. A sense of powerlessness ensues when you do not choose and keep mulling over the various options. To take ownership, or control, means to choose. To make choices and act on those choices, which is to choose to pursue change. Or to accept the situation as it is. Or to leave. When you choose, you regain control of your own feelings and behavior. And this will make you feel strong and more mature.

- Aidan could see if he can find a way to not take feedback so personally. If he manages that, he couldAnswer 'yes' to the question 'Can you change it?' and put some effort into achieving it.
- Georgia cannot change the attitude of others, but she can ask herself if she can accept that people are different. Perhaps she will then realize that her co-workers had no malicious intentions at all, and perhaps she will even realize that it is not even that bad to not be involved in everything.
- Peter cannot change the organizational culture at his company. He does not want to leave either, due to his age and financial situation. So, all that remains is to accept it.

The choice to change, accept, or leave always means that you also choose to behave accordingly, to change your behavior. If you do so, the situation will be less frustrating for you in the future. What is important, however, is that this new behavior will be behavior that is better aligned with your values (more about values in Chapter 4). To change, accept, or leave means that you take control, so that you feel better, are able to do what matters to you, and stay true to your values.

- Aidan opted to work on how he dealt with criticism, entirely in line with one of his values, personal development.
- Georgia would like a better working relationship with her co-workers. Accepting that others are different and still taking steps toward improving the working relationship helped her more than distancing herself from them in anger. It also better matches her value of having good working relationships with co-workers.
- Peter turned his annoyance into a positive by joining a sounding board group and take a constructive approach instead of continuing to moan about the corporate culture. It ultimately helped him get closer to his values of collaboration and positivity.

- What do you moan or complain about sometimes?
- If you wanted to take greater control of this situation, what step would you take (change, accept or leave)?

2.3   Keeping Your Eye on the Bigger Picture

Now you know which leadership styles there are and when to use them, and how to take ownership under all circumstances, the time has come to take a look at another important leadership skill. As a manager, it is crucially important that you never lose sight of the bigger picture. You need to have an ability to rise above the details and keep monitoring compliance with the company's strategy. And you need an ability to control your feelings (such as sympathy or a dislike toward certain people) and your intervention reflexes.

To see the bigger picture, you have to maintain a helicopter view at all time. This allows you to see what is happening from a distance, as you keep an eye on whether or not you are acting in the company's best interest, which allows you to stay flexible. A good manager monitors progress on the company's and team's goals and conformity to the company's and team's values.

In your leadership position, you must keep your eye on the bigger picture. Even when you feel upset because not all co-workers are cooperating. Even when your spirits are low. Even when you feel attacked or disappointed. But how do you still see the bigger picture in such situations?

1. You need to have the company's strategy top of mind, the ultimate goal for your company and your team. You need to know the values and be able to explain them to others. If you are unable to work from this starting position, chances are that you will be at the mercy of whatever arises when it arises.

2. You need to know yourself and be aware of your reflexes, your issues, and your weaknesses (see Chapter 7 on reflexes). When do you tend to lose sight of the bigger picture? And when do you feel small and unseen?

3. If you are able toAnswer these questions, you can defuse your reflexes. 'To defuse' is a concept that coaches and psychologists use to mean 'to separate yourself from something' (the opposite of 'to fuse'). It consists in realizing that you have certain reflexes and personal beliefs, but not acting on them. Or in being able to identify your pitfalls and reflexes, while still keeping your eye on the goal. Or in realizing that you want to be the rescuer of the situation but managing to regain your composure and stay focused.

If you are able to view your own work, actions, and attitude from a distance in this way, you will also be able to, from a mature mindset, consciously choose action that serves the greater goal.

- In which situations do you find that you are not focusing on the bigger picture but distracted by details?
- What could you do to prevent this from happening?

2.4   Conversation Skills for Mature Leadership

As a manager, you have all kinds of talks with your employees. Later on in this book, you will find guidelines on how to confront others respectfully and how to, for example, deliver bad news. Still, mature leadership also means you need a number of basic conversational skills. These are skills you will be able to deploy in nearly all cases to get a conversation of equals going with your employee.

Three Positions

To begin with, it is important that you be able to 'maintain a helicopter' view during a conversation. This is all about seeing the bigger picture, but now specifically the bigger picture of the conversation. In the following, I will explain how to maintain a helicopter view. You can approach a situation from three perspectives:

1. *From your own perspective:* you are constantly aware of your thoughts, behavior, feelings, and experience.
2. *From the other's perspective:* you are basically getting into your employee's head and asking yourself, 'What is the employee's take on the situation and how does the employee feel, think, and respond?'
3. *From the perspective of an objective observer:* while adopting the above perspectives, you also adopt a neutral perspective to assess what is happening in the interaction between you and the other.

Responding in a mature manner to what your employee does or says is a continuous balancing act between these three perspectives. You listen to your employee and sense what effect the employee's story, tone of voice, and behavior is having on you. This information helps you speak about the here-and-now instead of about the there-and-then. You are, as it were, standing beside your employee as an equal. The idea is to see into the employee's head and feel what it is like to be him or her, or to put yourself in his or her shoes. When you look at the world through your employee's eyes, you are empathizing. This will allow you to tune the conversation to your employee's reality, so that your employee feels understood and respected. And finally, a mature mindset means to be aware of how the interaction between the two of you develops. You are monitoring the conversation 'from up high in your helicopter.' This will also make you aware of the effect your words are having on your employee. Or how you respond to your employee. You are viewing from a distance what is happening between the two of you.

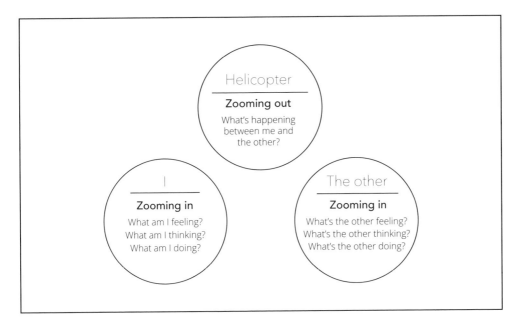

Figure 2.3   Three positions

Sometimes, you lose yourself in your own feelings, just like you can lose yourself in a friend. When you feel insecure or have all kinds of opinions about your employee, you are caught up in your own things and unable to listen properly. Still, you could also lose yourself in your employee's story too much, and subsequently forget to stay in control of the conversation and identify patterns. When that happens, you have simply projected yourself into the other too much. You are overdoing it on the empathy, and consequently no longer able to think and reflect clearly. And finally, you could also be cooped up in your helicopter too much and have completely ceased to feel the effect the conversation is having on you, because you have created too much distance.

I used to have an employee, Gwen, who often had conflicts with people in her immediate environment. Whenever I spoke to her about it, it was striking how angry and aggrieved she could get in response to situations, to co-workers who didn't think, to our secretary who didn't do enough, to fellow mothers at her child's school who behaved irresponsibly, and much more.

I felt her anger and ultimately got irritated myself by the things she described. I made a conscious decision to step away from my personal feelings and project myself into a different perspective, hers. I empathized and tried to feel what it must be like for her. She always felt responsible, was unable to let go, and felt she was surrounded by people cutting corners. She worked hard but felt that no one ever noticed her.

Next, I switched to the helicopter view. From up there, I saw two persons, Gwen and myself. She craved recognition, and I disengaged. Like so many others had done before me, tuning out because she always complained so much. In the end, she never got what she longed for, a genuine bond. The instant that I became able to view her this way, I was able to adopt a kinder mindset toward her and be more interested in her and listen to her. I was subsequently able to tell her, as her equal, what effect her negativity tended to have on others. Without judging her, purely out of a desire to help her develop.

Listen, Recap, and Keep Asking Questions

To get a conversation of equals going, it is important, and this goes without saying, that you be a good listener. It may sound like stating the obvious, but you would be surprised how hard active listening actually is. Active listening is a technique that is made up of three elements: to listen, to recap, and to keep asking questions.

Listen

By listening, you are focusing your attention on the other, allowing and encouraging them to tell their story. But listening is not only about passively hearing what the other has to say. If you listen actively, you are not only paying attention to what someone says, but also to how they say it, their tone of voice, volume, and body language. You can show the other that you are actively listening by adopting an open and active posture, nodding and uh-huhing, not being afraid of silences, and by maintaining eye contact.

Recap

There are various ways to recap:

- Recapping to motivate the other to keep talking. For example: 'So you thought that meeting went well?'
- Recapping to verify whether you understood the other correctly. For example: 'Correct me if I'm wrong, but you would like to be put on a different project.'
- And recapping to close a certain topic or the whole conversation. This is a kind of rundown to confirm what you discussed or to make sure agreements are clear. For example: 'OK, so we've looked at the schedule. Is it correct that we have agreed that you will talk to HR about publishing a vacancy in the short term?'

Recaps are brief and to-the-point reflections of the core of the other's story. Try to recap in your own words as much as possible, except when you feel that you are dealing with a delicate matter. If that is the case, you would be better off phrasing the recap using the other's words. Try to use neutral words, so as not to put your own personal spin on the summary.

You can recap content and feelings. Recapping content speaks for itself, because you merely repeat what your employee said in your own words. When recapping feelings, you go one step further, as you try to guess what the other is feeling. You are then pinpointing a feeling that the employee has not made explicit, but which you have picked up on between the lines or based on the way the other spoke about it. For example, first recap the content ('So you thought it wasn't a good idea to assign Pien that task') and then describe the feeling you picked up on ('And it seems to me that you felt frustrated and concerned, is that right?'). It does not actually matter if your guess is off the mark. If it is, your employee will correct you soon enough and tell how he or she really felt.

Keep Asking Questions

You need to look for leads for further questioning. What do you mean? Why did you think that? What is keeping you? This is when you look for things to latch onto or inconsistencies in your employee's story, things you can get your employee to expand on.

To keep asking questions is to ask for further explanation of what the other already told you. This will give you a better idea of the other's facts, ideas, opinions, and feelings. You can ask further questions to cover a greater breadth of different topics, or to go in depth, asking about details of specific matters. When you keep asking questions, you are encouraging the other to share more and you get a better idea of what the other is trying to tell you.

Silences

One key listening skill is the ability to tolerate silences, which is far from easy. The thing is that if you immediately start talking when the other stops talking, you are taking over; that is when the mother speaks, driven by an urge to help the other. And the other will then think, 'Ah, she didn't understand my question, or she doesn't know theAnswer.' Or it is the macho taking over. The macho who knows best or who wants to speed up the conversation.

When you are in mature mode when listening to the other, you will not have this urge to fill silences, thus allowing the other to think about anAnswer or find the right words. In fact, if you ask a question that your employee has to think about, it is probably a very good question, one that can produce real insight. But when you immediately start talking to fill the silence, you are wasting this opportunity for understanding.

Staying in Control of the Conversation

Keeping a distance and listening, recapping, and asking further questions is not enough. As a manager, you also want to have a certain level of control of a conversation. Does the following sound familiar? You are in a conversation that is taking longer than you had planned and you think, 'This has gone very differently from what I envisioned.' The steps in Figure 2.4 will help you stay in control of the direction in which a conversation is headed. Without dictating the content, it allows you to stay in charge of the structure of the conversation.

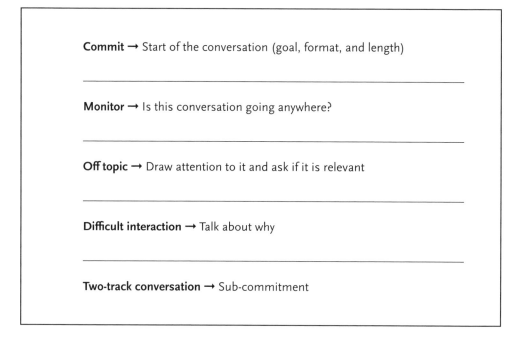

Commit → Start of the conversation (goal, format, and length)

Monitor → Is this conversation going anywhere?

Off topic → Draw attention to it and ask if it is relevant

Difficult interaction → Talk about why

Two-track conversation → Sub-commitment

Figure 2.4   Staying in Control of the Conversation

Commit: Start of the Conversation (Goal, Format, and Length)

By making clear mutual commitments at the start of the conversation, you make sure you and your employee are on the same wavelength in terms of what you will be discussing. Without realizing it, many conversations start without setting a clear goal at the start. Even when your employee has come into your office unannounced, it is a good idea to first quickly figure out what exactly your employee wants from you - before you slip into the mother or macho role and start solving the problem (also refer to the section on 'walk-ins' in 6.1). Questions to ask during the commitment stage include:

- What is the objective of this conversation? Is this what you wanted to talk about?
- What do you want to achieve with this conversation?
- Do you want to look for a solution or figure out how it happened in the first place?

Monitor: Is This Conversation Going Anywhere?

Do you sometimes think while talking to your employee, 'Is this helping my employee in any way? 'Is what I am saying actually relevant to my employee?' If so, just ask. You could ask:

- Is this what you had in mind?
- Does it help you to talk about this?
- Would it make sense to keep talking about this?

Off Topic: Draw Attention to It and Ask If It Is Relevant

Conversations often do not adhere to a fixed structure. You may start talking about your employee's health and before you know it, you are talking about something else entirely. If you notice that you are going off topic, talking about something other than what you had agreed to talk about, draw attention to it, do not just accept it.

If you are having a conversation because you wanted to talk about something in particular, you can steer the conversation back to the original subject. During a coaching session, you could ask your employee whether the subject that is off topic might also be relevant.

Difficult Interaction: Talk about Why

When the interaction is tough going, make sure you address this. Difficult interaction can come in many different manifestations, such as bluntness in your employee's responses or a mutual urge to try to convince the other, meaning that you have stopped listening to each other. Discuss what you are experiencing and ask how your employee feels about it. You could say:

- Gee, this conversation is not going smoothly at all, is it?
- Wow, yourAnswers are really short, what's up?
- I'm noticing that we are both trying to persuade each other of our ideas, we often do that. Have you noticed that as well?
- It seems like I always have to come up with the solutions to your problems. Is that something you recognize?
- Ever since I brought up the new project, you seem irritable and you barely respond. Is there something the matter?

Two-Track Conversation: Sub-Commitment

Conversations can also veer off into two different directions, creating a two-track conversation. This happens when you hear your employee say two different things, such as that he or she gets nervous when giving presentations and does not like being in the spotlight at all. When that happens, you need to agree on a sub-commitment and ask your employee, 'Do you want to discuss both these things or is it essentially one subject? And if you want to explore both, where do you want to start?' Through such a mutual sub-commitment during the conversation, you are staying in control of the conversation.

> Your employee comes to talk to you about her problems with the IT department. You ask her what she wants to do about her problems, to which she replies that she wants better communication with them, and so you recap, 'Okay, so we are going to discuss what you can do to ensure smoother communication with IT.' (This is the commitment step, to agree on a goal for the conversation.) Later during the conversation, you hear her say, 'Things are basically the same with sales support, I also feel that I'm not getting through to them either.' The subject of your conversation could then become how she can more effectively influence the various departments. You could ask her to pick a subject and talk about communication with the IT department or about exerting influence in general. Being clear about what you are going to talk about will prevent time wastage.

- Think back to a conversation that you thought was difficult and go over the three perspectives. What did YOU think and feel?
- And now the other. What do you think the other thought and felt?
- And finally, from the helicopter perspective, what did you see happen between you? What were you doing and what effect did it have on the other and vice versa?
- In terms of 'staying in control of the conversation,' could you have done anything differently during that conversation?
- During your next conversation, try to recap what the other is saying. And subsequently recap the other's feelings as well. What effect does this have?

2.5   Summary

I have used the theory of situational leadership to show that you can make an assessment of how good your employee already is at a certain task, and how much self-confidence your employee already has. Based on this assessment, you can choose whether to instruct, persuade, coach, or delegate, allowing you to pick and choose leadership styles based on each specific task.

The Control Model shows how you, as a manager, can take ownership, even when things are not going your way. In such situations, you can start complaining and rebelling, but that will generally not make you feel any better. What will make you feel better is if you take ownership of the situation, if you take control. You always have a choice. You can change the situation, accept it, or leave. Choosing any of these three options, and behaving accordingly, will give you a sense of control. On top of that, it will ensure that you stay true to your values, to the values that are important to you.

There are several conversation techniques that can help you, as a leader, manager, and coach, to take a mature approach to a situation. Assuming a helicopter view, which means to view yourself, the other, and your interaction from a distance, will enable you to identify patterns and break out of those patterns. And active listening, recapping, and asking further questions will help you create open and honest interaction with your employee. You can stay in control of your conversations by committing to a topic to discuss and by, for example, being open about a conversation not going smoothly, instead of sweeping it under the carpet. Or by not letting your employee change the subject unchallenged.

3   Leader, Manager, Coach

Many of today's managers have ended up in a position of leadership more or less by accident. The company where you work may grow at such a rate that new leadership positions are added all the time, or you may be a stand-in for a manager on a temporary basis or have temporarily been assigned an employee to supervise. But you may also have been asked to take on a leadership position simply because you are the best worker on your team. Or perhaps you have applied for a leadership role or you got into it by chance. Whatever got you into your leadership position, the thing now is to actually do it, to go and lead, manage, and coach.

There is no role that draws on so many different competencies as a leadership position. And yet, many (starting) managers get little support in this area. A move into leadership is a major change, as you suddenly have to set a good example. Where you used to maybe join co-workers for drinks and gossip about the management team, you now have to watch what you say. You have to keep some of the things you see or experience to yourself. You no longer feel you are one of them. And the fact is, you no longer are one of them.

During a training program for new managers, one student, Robert, tells us that he currently heads up a team that he used to be a member of. He now reports to the managing director, whom he used to moan about quite a lot. He used to do a lot of gossiping with his fellow team members about the poor quality of management. But now, being a manager himself and attending the weekly management team meeting, he sometimes feels a bit lonely. He can no longer gossip about the board with his co-workers, while his fellow management team members do not quite feel like his equals yet either.

Nancy's company kept growing and growing, until she noticed that no matter what employees asked her, it always irritated her. She took a step back to reflect on what was going on. She concluded that dealing with employees who are having problems is difficult and a major energy drain for her. This is something she wants to change. She decided to take coaching leadership training to learn to waste less energy in managing people. And to take more time to develop new concepts, because that is what she is passionate about.

3.1 The Roles of Leader, Manager, and Coach

In leadership, there are basically three different roles (see Figure 3.1).
- The leader role
- The manager role
- The coach role

It is advisable to regularly make a conscious choice as to what role to use for a specific purpose.

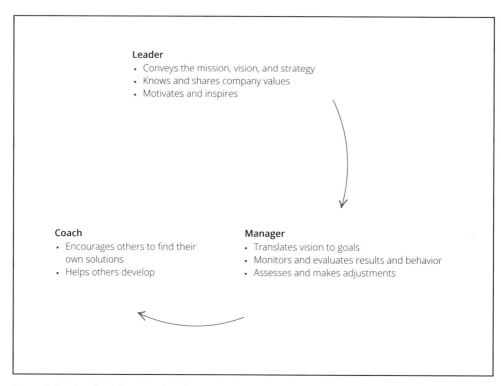

Leader
- Conveys the mission, vision, and strategy
- Knows and shares company values
- Motivates and inspires

Coach
- Encourages others to find their own solutions
- Helps others develop

Manager
- Translates vision to goals
- Monitors and evaluates results and behavior
- Assesses and makes adjustments

Figure 3.1   Leader, Manager, Coach

The Leader Role
- Conveys the mission, vision, and strategy
- Knows and shares company values
- Motivates and inspires

Before you delve into your management tasks (setting goals, handling performance reviews, etc.) and coaching tasks (helping your employees develop), it is key that you be a good leader first, that you instill the company's vision and mission in your employees' minds. This is because it is important that employees know where the company is headed, what the long-term goals are, what the vision for the future is, and what strategy is supposed to get the company there. At most companies, the board defines the vision, but sometimes you can formulate a vision as a group of managers or employees, depending on the size of the company. No matter who defined the vision, it is your responsibility as a leader to ensure that your team has it top of mind. The leader role is the subject of Chapter 4.

The Manager Role
- Translates vision to goals
- Monitors results and behavior
- Assesses and makes adjustments

Once it is clear where you as a company or department are headed, you can translate this to what you expect from your employees. In the manager role, you set the goals for your team and individual employees. You give your team actual responsibility for their targets by asking them what their targets should be, asking them how they think they can help the company achieve its goals. When the goals are clear, it is your job to monitor progress on achieving them. Are some of the results not quite what they should be, are we focusing on the right things? In the manager role, you look at both the results your employees achieve and at their behavior, at how they work. You conduct performance reviews and also make sure employees are called to account on their performance between reviews. More about the manager role in Chapter 5.

The Coach Role
- Encourages others to find their own solutions
- Helps others develop

When you have made your employee aware of development needs, or your employee comes to you for help in pursuing development, you can use coaching skills to help your employee change. How to apply the coaching role will be explained in Chapter 6.

When it comes to sequentiality, there is no fixed sequence of roles. In practice, they are alternated without a particular pattern. You may even find yourself being a coach one minute and sharing a vision document the next. What is important, however, is to make sure you are always clear in sharing your expectations. After all, if you were to start coaching without having shared your expectations and the vision, you may end up coaching your employee in one direction and seeing your employee develop in another direction.

> During a performance review, your employee tells you that she wants to become an expert in a specific area. She would like to see her task load reduced and focus more on one specific task.
>
> You, however, want your employees to be deployable to a broader range of tasks, as you want every account manager to be able to serve multiple clients. Your employee's coaching need clashes with your vision and plans. By regularly making time to share your vision, you can prevent these kinds of situations where you find out after a coaching session that your employee has development goals that do not match what you have in mind for your employee.

Most of us who work in leadership have a preferred role. Many admit that they simply cannot find the time for the leader role in the everyday hustle and bustle. During my leadership training sessions, participants realize that they sometimes mistakenly assume that their employees are already familiar with the company's mission and vision.

Others struggle with the manager role, finding it hard to get their expectations across and conduct performance reviews. You have to dare to be straight with employees; some managers prefer to duck difficult conversations.

I also know people in leadership positions who find the coach role the one that requires the most effort. They dread having to calmly and emphatically listen to an employee, thinking that coaching is too time consuming. And they are not always able to muster the patience to transfer responsibility to the employee. They often slip into the more directing role of the manager (macho).

> - How did you end up in a leadership position? Was it your ambition or did it just happen?
> - What do you like about your leadership position? And what do you not like about it?
> - Which role do you find the easiest to fulfill? And which one the hardest? Why?

3.2 Summary

In a leadership position, you basically have to fulfill three different roles: the role of leader, the role of manager, and the role of coach. It is advisable to regularly make a conscious choice as to what role to use for a specific purpose.

Always make sure you first cover the tasks that go with the leader role, which is to convey the company's mission, vision, and strategy, and to know the company's values and share them with your team. The ultimate goal of the leader role is to motivate and inspire your employees. In the manager role, you set targets for your employees, you monitor progress, evaluate, and make adjustments. In the coach role, finally, you encourage your employees to find their own solutions and you help them develop.

The next three chapters will each be dedicated to one of these three roles.

4   Leader

When fulfilling a leadership position, you have to be a leader, a manager, and a coach. You need all these three roles. This chapter is about your role as leader. It is about what this role entails, what skills and tasks go with it, and what pitfalls you may come up against.

In the leader role, you need to be able to maintain an overview and see the bigger picture and manage to get your employees to commit to the preferred direction, in a way that makes that your employees want to follow you. Your enthusiasm needs to rub off on them. You will be a strong leader if you are trustworthy and authentic - and if you stay true to your values. Whenever you are having difficulty managing or coaching your employees, first ask yourself whether you have been clear in your leader role. If you have not, focus on tasks such as conveying the company's mission, vision, and strategy first, as well as on sharing the company values.

4.1   Leader: Conveys the Mission, Vision, and Strategy

What is perhaps the most important skill for a leader is the ability to define and/or convey the company's mission, vision, and strategy. If you are not the managing director, the mission and vision will most likely already have been defined for you. There will generally be an outline of a corporate strategy, which you are expected to work out further for your department or team.

How Do You Do That?
If you want committed employees, it is key that you share with them what the company or department wants to work toward. Keep raising awareness of the company's goals. And check with your employees what they think is the goal for your company and department. On team-building days, for example, devote time to this by organizing a session where you all describe your department's goal together. When welcoming new hires to the team or when there are changes on the team, you should pay extra attention to this.

Emilia is branch manager at a large staffing agency and has enrolled in a leadership program. During the part about the three different roles, she realizes that she doesn't use the leader role very often. She assumed that the annual company kick-off meeting was enough to get the strategy across to everyone. After the training, she decided to check this at the first meeting she had. As it turned out, most of the members of her team were unable to tell her what the company's mission and vision is, and the strategy wasn't entirely clear to them either. Together with her team, she came up with a plan to raise awareness. She invited one of the members of the board to come and explain the company's mission, vision, and strategy. Ultimately, she agreed with the team to theme each month on one of the company's specific core values. And the new-hire induction program now includes time to share the mission, vision, and strategy,

- What is your organization's mission and vision?
- What is your department's/team's goal?
- How do you share the mission, vision, and goals with your employees?

Pitfalls

- Strategy is hassle

You lack the time to focus on strategy, and you do not make enough time for it. Maybe you are not a great forward thinker by nature. Or perhaps the mere mention of the word 'strategy' makes you feel anxious or insecure. 'Strategy' also tends to sound somewhat pompous. It could also be that you feel that you have little influence over strategy or that formulating a mission and vision is always pointless because they generally end up on a shelf somewhere never to be looked at again.

- It is not my vision

You do not support the vision and strategy, or you do not believe in it. The company you work for is, in your view, overly focused on financial gains, while you find your employees' personal development more important. Or your organization claims to be environmentally responsible, but you do not see it reflected in the company's day-to-day operations. In both cases, you find it hard to convey the strategy.

- They have no strategy

I often hear managers complain about their board or management team, bemoaning a lack of vision or the absence of a strategy. They feel that the board falls short when there is no clear mission, vision, and strategy. Or they think the current vision could do with a rethink or should be put to paper unequivocally.

Avoiding Pitfalls

When you moan, you are not taking ownership. This is when you are in the bottom half of the Control Model (Section 2.2). You are fighting against your reality and judging it. Moaning does not fit in a mature leadership style. Taking ownership does. Therefore, make time to define your own personal strategy, no matter how difficult this is for you. If you cannot find it in yourself to back your company's strategy, do not hide it, but talk about it. If a clearly defined strategy is lacking or the strategy is out of date, write one yourself and submit it to your board. There is always something you can do to get clarity on your company's mission, vision, and strategy. And if there is nothing you can change and you cannot accept the strategy, the only option that remains is to leave.

4.2   Leader: Knows and Shares the Company's Values

An organization not only has a mission and a goal, it also has values. A value is a principle that your organization considers worthy of pursuit. A value is a judgment of what is important, such as good behavior. Values transmit the corporate culture and they do not change every year. They are reasonably clear-cut and run through the company's veins. A company's values are often formulated or defined by the management. Some companies put them to paper or on their company website and then largely disregard them, but others have clearly defined values that underlie their operations, as is the case at companies such as Disney and McDonald's, for example. Values are not about your product or service, but about the mindset at your company, the corporate culture, the intrinsic values of the people working for your company.

How Do You Do That?

As a leader, you must first make sure you are fully aware of the company's values. If you are not, make sure values are formulated and then represent these values toward your people. After all, values will only serve a purpose when they are reflected in everything your organization says and does. Values should not merely be a few bullet points in the corporate brochure, they must also come across in how you approach customers and in your HR policy. This is where you come in, because you are the role model when it comes to values. Always make sure that your personal working practices and the way you communicate are in sync with your company's values. An effective way to bring values to life is to brainstorm together with your employees about how these values drive the various aspects of your operations.

Even when they have never been put to paper, your company still has values. To identify them, you can often go back to the beginnings of the company and its founder(s). What was important at the time and what did they find important? Why and how did this company come to be? You can also look at what kind of behavior the company seeks to foment. What kind of behavior is considered exemplary and how do employees treat each other?

- What are your company's values? You might find them in your company's mission statement. If not, hazard a guess.
- Regardless of whether or not values have been defined, what is considered important at your company? What do board members/higher executives look at?
- What values do you see reflected in most employees' behavior?
- Are the aboveAnswers aligned in any way? If not, what is the main difference between them?

Personal Values

It's not only your organization that has values. You do too. What do you find important in life? What values are truly yours, and not only socially desirable and/or professionally relevant? Values differ from one person to the next. Where one person may feel strongly about compassion, another may well find freedom or autonomy very important. Our values and the importance we attach to them are what makes us unique. Values also set your standards and drive your behavior, as they capture what you pursue in life or how you want to behave. When you are true to your values in life, you will be happier and feel better. Your values are your foundation. They are generally shaped during childhood, forged through a combination of life experience and culture or social environment. Although your values tend to be stable, they can still be shaken by (impactful) events and experiences.

How do you figure out what your personal values are? Values are not the same as life goals. Contrary to values, goals can be achieved and checked off a list. A possible value could be 'to have a healthy lifestyle,' which is never 'done,' as it is something you have to pursue your whole life. 'To lose weight,' however, and 'to run a marathon' are life goals you can check off as soon as you have achieved them.

Three Exercises to Determine your Personal Values

1. *Questions to get an idea of your personal values*
   What do you truly want? What is truly important to you in life?
   Imagine you won the lottery. What would you take up, and what would you quit?
   What makes you happy? What can they wake you up for in the middle of the night?

2. *The actually list*
   Write down what you would 'actually' want to do, but never got around to doing.

3. *Start by focusing on the end*
   Write a letter to yourself from the future. Imagine you have reached the ripe old age of 80 and are telling your younger self what has been important in your life. What have you done, what fills you with pride, and what was, in hindsight, less successful? What made you happy?

If you work at a company with values that match yours, you will feel committed to the company. But the values of the company may not be so well-aligned with yours.

Pitfalls

- Conflicting values

There could also be a disconnect between your company's values and your personal values, which may cause you to struggle to get the company's value across to your people, simply because you (actually) feel differently.

One value that Lena considers very important is personal development. Being able to develop herself, use her talents, and achieve inner growth is what's important to her and what she enjoys. The dynamic startup where she is one of the managers consumes all her time and focus. As a result, she was forced to skip a course she would have liked to take. Gradually, she realizes that her personal development has stalled. It is slowly becoming painful to her that this personal value is featuring so little in her life.

For Nicholas, having a relaxed laid-back lifestyle is what matters most. He is currently on the management team of a company where everyone works a lot of overtime. He, too, is expected to work evenings and weekends. Nicholas works extremely long days. One day, he realizes that he's not happy, as the work pace and workplace atmosphere at his company are increasingly stressing him out.

For Paul, taking good care of oneself is a key value in life. At the company where he works, however, employee wellbeing is way down on the list of priorities. More and more often, Paul finds, when having certain talks with his employees, that his heart isn't in it, as he has to tell his employees things that do not chime with his personal values. One example was when the company wouldn't let him renew the contract of an employee who wanted to cut his working week to four days after the birth of his first child. In the end, Paul concluded that the company simply wasn't a good fit for him, and he resigned.

- 'They're not my values'

You cannot find it in yourself to endorse the values. They are not authentic, in your view, or you do not see them reflected in your company's operations. Some companies formulate their values in extremely abstract terms, making them almost incomprehensible.

- 'They have no values'

Another possible situation is that the company you work for does not have a clearly defined set of values (yet). This does not mean they do not have values, it merely means they have not been put to paper yet.

Avoiding Pitfalls

The same as described earlier in reference to the mission, vision, and strategy applies to values as well. If you do not agree with your company's values, you might feel trapped. It may prompt you to look for some elbow room to be able to stay true to yourself. Think back to the Control Model (Section 2.2). Can you change the situation? If you have any kind of control over your company's values, take ownership and shape them, express your opinion and help write a document that specifies the values in clear terms. If this is not an option, all you can do is accept it or leave.

4.3   Leader: Motivates and Inspires

A key aspect of your leader role is to engage employees to buy into your message, so as to be able to motivate them. If yours is an authentic, credible message, one that you clearly stand behind, employees will like listening to you and believe you.

How Do You Do That?

• Make your message personal and authentic

Invite your employees to join your thought process. Instead of only sharing your conclusions, also share your reasoning in arriving at your conclusions. Why did you choose this strategy and not another? Why does this value or statement take center stage? What does it mean to you personally? The more you share about what it means to you personally, the more your message will hit home.

• The power of repetition

It may sound obvious, but messages that people are confronted with repeatedly in different ways are the ones they remember. Your message will not instantly sink in with everyone in the same way. A good leader takes time to repeat a message and make it connect. Therefore, make sure you communicate the things that matter to you often and in different ways. You could capture your strategy in visuals, put your brand values up on the wall, or jointly work out departmental goals.

• Appreciation

And to state the obvious again, your employees want to feel appreciated. They want to feel appreciated by you, by the company. People need a sense of purpose. To motivate your employees, make sure they feel noticed. The best way to do

that is to genuinely pay attention and listen to them, by letting them know that you have seen that they regularly put in overtime, work extra hours, or put extra effort into a project. Instead of leaving positives unsaid, tell your employee that you have noticed how he or she helped a colleague or compliment your employee on how well he or she prepared for a presentation. By keeping your eyes open and sharing what you have seen, you are showing your employee that they matter.

• Connection

You also need to know how to win employees over to your ideas and your vision. This is all about listening genuinely and managing to tap into what drives and motivates them. By taking employees' perspective, you can make sure your message connects. And creating this kind of connection will lead to commitment, as your employees feel at ease with you and at home at the company, and ultimately loyal to both.

Pitfalls

• You're just not doing it

There are all kinds of reasons (excuses) why you may fail to motivate and inspire employees. Perhaps you just forget to do it, cannot find the time to do it, or are not very good at it. Or you may be insecure about it, or simply believe that your employees should self-motivate.

• You are too eager to persuade

Perhaps you are the type of person who is quick to try to start persuading people, or the type of person who starts to try to persuade people when sensing they have doubts about the message. Many will be aware of this pitfall. As soon as you notice resistance or hesitation, the persuader in you goes into overdrive, hoping that your arguments will win over your employees. You think that they will come over to your views by hearing your arguments once again. The macho role clearly comes to the fore in this tendency to persuade.

> On many occasions, I tried to convince my employees that they should consider organizational changes or a new project as an opportunity. I sometimes noticed resistance among team members whenever yet another new project was launched. It was not clear to me what it was that bothered them, but I suspected it was the increased workload. I thought this was a silly knee-jerk reaction on their part, as I wanted them to see the commercial opportunities. So, I switched to persuasion mode, highlighting the benefits of the project, making it clear that it was the best way to reach greater numbers of people and ultimately hit our target. I basically kept persuading until I had silenced the resistance. But what I never figured out is where the resistance came from in the first place, because I never asked anyone about it, I merely crushed the resistance with my persuasion skills, so I thought.

Avoiding Pitfalls

If you are just not doing the whole motivating your employees thing, ask yourself what is keeping you. Why are you not doing it and what will help you start doing it?

If you are overly eager to motivate, you should mix up your communication styles. If you see that your plans, your strategy, or brand values have not really connected with your employees explore why that is the case, instead of firing (more) arguments at them. Find out why they are not getting it, or why they reject your message. Ask open, curious questions, recap their feelings to give them the opportunity to tell you what is bothering them.

When you want your employees to share, curb your critical (macho) side and turn on mature mode. Show understanding and let your employees know that it is okay to have doubts, hesitate, discuss. Only if you have a solid understanding of why your employees do not share or accept your opinion can you start thinking about how to remove their doubts, how to turn their incomprehension into comprehension, or perhaps even to rethink or improve your own views. Customize your approach to the people you are talking to and their level, job, or role.

Your motivational efforts will be most effective if you connect with your employees. So, engage with their interests and motivation. What does your plan/strategy mean for your team? Does it enable your colleagues to achieve their goals? Will it make their work easier? In other words, *what's in it for them?*

> - What is your main development need in the leader role?
> - What would you like to do more of?
> - Which pitfalls do you recognize? Is there anything you want to do about that?

4.4   Summary

This chapter is about the leader's three tasks, as well as the leader's pitfalls and how to avoid them.

1. *A leader conveys the mission, vision, and strategy*
Pitfall: you don't devote enough time to it. It just seems like hassle to you, you feel insecure doing it, you do not endorse the strategy, or you do not believe in it. Sometimes, a strategy is lacking altogether.
Mature: you take ownership of it.

2. *A leader knows and shares the company's values*
Pitfall: you have a personal take on the company's values. They do not match your own, making it hard for you to convey them. Or you do not find them authentic. Or you have no idea what the company's values are.
Mature: you take control. Can you change the situation? If you can, do it. If not, you can choose, accept the situation or leave.

3. *A leader motivates and inspires*

Pitfall: you're not doing it or you're trying to persuade your employees.

Mature: you figure out what is stopping you, or why your employees are reluctant to connect with your message. Show understanding. Engage with their interests and motivation.

5 Manager

This chapter is about the manager role. The manager is the one who translates the vision and strategy conveyed by the leader to specific goals and targets. What exactly do you expect from your department and your employees? In the manager role, you formulate expectations and set goals, but that is not the end of it. After that, you have to monitor, adjust goals or agreements, hold your employees accountable and assess their performance and the results.

5.1   Manager: Translates Vision into Goals

In the role of manager, you translate the vision and strategy you established or conveyed in the leader role into goals for your department or team, as well as into goals for individual employees. You define what exactly you expect from each employee and how each employee can help the company achieve its objectives and realize its vision.

How Do You Do That?
Based on the chosen vision, you set the goals for the coming year, 18 months, 5 years, or any other period. You can set these goals yourself by assessing what your employees need to do to achieve the desired outcome, but what is more effective is to give your employees a say in formulating the goals. Letting your employees define goals themselves or at least giving them a role in defining goals will create greater commitment on their part.

Pitfalls
- Wanting to be liked

Something you may come up against in setting goals is that your desire to be liked leads to you postponing this part of your job or not doing it unequivocally. Some managers try to avoid being overly demanding on their employees, or even go easy on them altogether (mother role). The pitfall you will then run into is that you are not clear on what exactly you expect from your employees.

Theresa just started out in a leadership role at a department of administrators. During a leadership training session, she shares that she herself was set rather steep goals. Her department needs to become considerably more professional. Her employees have been complaining about work pressure for some time now and some instantly show their disapproval whenever Theresa asks them to do something. The training opens her eyes to the fact that although she told her employees all about the board's plans, she never specifically told the team what she expects from them. She never made any specific agreements on targets. Simply because she is anxious about how her team might react, she always avoided the subject.

- Overambitious

Another pitfall that looms large is that your goals are overambitious. There is nothing as demotivating to employees as being set unattainable goals. If you know right away that something is unachievable, you will simply not even try.

Avoiding Pitfalls

In a mature mindset, you rely on your employees to be able to decide for themselves how they will contribute to achieving the desired result. As soon as you notice that your employees set themselves either easy or unachievable targets, you can talk about it by being open and honest about your observations.

You can always help employees formulate clear goals, supporting them in setting feasible goals that match their level. The idea must always be to formulate goals based on the SMART criteria (Specific, Measurable, Attainable, Realistic, Time-bound), so that it is clear to you and your employees what they will be assessed on.

- What are your department's goals?
- Does every employee know what their contribution to these goals is?

5.2   Manager: Monitors and Reviews Results and Behavior

Once the objectives for your team and each individual employee are clear and have been shared with your employees, it is up to you to monitor progress and review the results. When results fail to materialize, it is your job to talk to your employees about it. Besides monitoring progress and results, the manager role also involves keeping an eye on your employees' behavior.

How Do You Do That?

How to monitor progress and results differs from one company to the next. Many organizations have a management information system, but it may well be that results are plain to see without the help of a performance tracking system. Regardless of how it is done at your company, being the manager means that you need to stay on top of how things are going. Given that you must regularly discuss results with your employees, you could decide to make this a fixture on the agenda for meetings. Again, in the manager role, you tell your employee what is expected of him or her, while allowing the employee to come up with his or her own solutions to make up arrears.

As a manager, you not only have result expectations, you also have behavioral expectations, which are expectations with respect to how your employee does things such as work together with others, communicate, and identify opportunities. It is crucial that your employee know exactly what behavior you expect him or her to display. What behavior suits your employee's role, also going forward. This should be formulated in as specific terms as possible.

At my training sessions, I often hear managers say, 'My employee is doing a great job, but his behavior leaves much to be desired.' They would say that in reference to, for example, a data analyst who analyzes all the data perfectly, but sometimes yells at co-workers. Or a recruiter who hits her targets, but whose negative attitude sours the work atmosphere. In these kinds of cases, my conclusion would be that the employees in question are simply not doing a good job. Although their results may be fine, performance is a combination of results and behavior. Therefore, to be satisfied with an employee's performance, an employee needs to do well on both fronts.

Respectful Confrontation

Whenever your employee fails to hit targets or you see behavior you consider unwanted, it is key that you talk to your employee about it. When doing that, the way you do it is crucial. It takes real skill not to slip into either the mother role or the macho role. You want to be straight with your employee about what you think, what you have seen, and what you feel, and you want to do that in a respectful manner. The idea is for your employee not to feel attacked or small, but for your employee to hear what you have to say and know what to do with your feedback. This kind of respectful confrontation is a tricky balancing act, but it is also one of the most important skills in coaching leadership.

When you confront your employee, your aim should be either to challenge your employee on counterproductive behavior (because you want to improve collaboration) or to correct behavior that is keeping your employee from developing (you want to help your employee improve). If you then state your intentions before you get into the actual conversation, your employee will know instantly what you are looking to get out of it. You could say, 'I'm going to tell you something you might not like to hear, but please realize that I'm doing it because it will help you improve the way you present yourself.' I will use the steps in Figure 5.1 to explain how to get respectful confrontation right.

Reflection
Is it an incident, accident, or a pattern?
Is it mine or the other's?

Step 1   Specific behavior
I see   The observation
I hear   The facts

Step 2   Effect
I think   The effect of the observation on my thinking
I feel   The effect of the observation on my emotions
I act   The effect of the observation on my behavior

Is this something you recognize?

Step 3   Request | Desire
               I would like to explore how we could deal with this
               I want to tell you this
               I would like you to do this differently

Note: If you are confronting the other because the other irritates you, make sure you also share your personal sensitivity that underlies this sensation of irritation.

Figure 5.1   Respectful Confrontation

Before You Begin: Reflect

Before you have a respectful confrontation talk, reflect on your situation. Briefly step back and look at yourself from the helicopter. Is what you are about to discuss an incident, an accident, or a pattern? If it is something that irritates you, it is probably a pattern. You should then ask yourself what pattern exactly you are seeing. What does your employee keep doing that irritates you or what impression does your employee keep making?

Next, ask yourself to what extent the irritation 'is your own doing' and to what extent it is triggered by your employee. Does your employee do something you would never do? Or does your employee do something that makes you jealous? These kinds of sentiments have a tendency to color your opinion.

Ask yourself these questions to briefly step out of the situation and take an objective look at it. This does not mean, however, that you should not have the talk if you conclude that most of the irritation is your own doing. Have the talk but take ownership of any of your own sensitivities that have led to the situation.

Step 1: Specific Behavior

The first step is to present your observation in specific terms, listing the facts without judgment and blame, to share what you have seen the employee do or heard the employee say. Describe it in a way that does not trigger debate, stick to the facts. To help you describe your employee's behavior in specific terms, try to imagine how a third person would perceive the behavior. Speak in the first person (I see, I hear) and use neutral language to make sure the employee does not feel judged.

Pitfall

One pitfall that looms large when describing your observation is that you lapse into assumptions and judgments. The observation in itself is a fact. But in practice, the observation often has an impact on you. For example: you regularly see an employee staring at their phone and you instantly think, 'He's texting all the time, he's not focusing on his work.' The second part is your assumption, not an observation. The following statements are not observations:

- I see you checking your phone all day. (assumption)
- You don't take me seriously. (assumption)
- I wonder if you even like your job. (assumption)
- You're always late. (judgment)

But what should you say instead? The following are examples of observations without judgment or assumptions:

- I can see that you came in after 9.15 on three occasions this week.
- I've noticed that you check your phone several times a day.
- I see that you're wiggling in your seat.

Note that words such as *always, never,* and *often* have a judgmental ring to them. Try to avoid using these kinds of words. But still try to be open and honest, there is no need to sugarcoat your observation.

Step 2: The Effect

The second step is to describe the effect on your thinking, feelings, and behavior. What are the consequences of the observation? What does it make you THINK, how does it make you FEEL, and how does it make you ACT?

Pitfalls

Sharing what you think about it is generally not that hard to do but pinpointing how it makes you feel is a lot harder. Merely starting a sentence by saying 'I feel that...' is not enough.

When you say, 'I feel that you don't know what you're talking about,' you are not describing your feeling, you are describing your thinking. It may sound like stating the obvious, but a feeling is something you FEEL, a sensation you physically feel in your body. There are four basic emotions: fear, anger, happiness, sadness. All feelings are effectively (light) versions of these basic emotions, such as agitated, feeling small, feeling lost, concerned.

While talking to your employee, he regularly checks his phone. You want to say something about it, because it bothers you. You can put the effect it is having on you into words as follows:

'I think that you find your phone more important than our conversation. It makes me feel agitated and I notice that I'm raising my voice to attract your attention.'

Intermediary Step: Is This Something You Recognize?

Next, ask your employee, 'Is this something you recognize?' or 'What is it like to hear this?' This way, you are giving your employee the opportunity to tell his or her side of the story. This step will introduce equality into the conversation, because if you only transmit and do not ask anything, you may come across as blunt and dominant (macho), making the other feel small and less likely to take ownership of their behavior.

Step 3: Request or Desire

The final step is your request to the employee. Do you want the other to change? Do you want to talk about it? What is it that you want in this case? Make sure you present your request as a genuine request (and not as a demand), because your request is your suggestion as to how to get closer to the goal. Perhaps your employee has another take on it and a different suggestion.

These three steps (observation, effect, request) kick off your conversation. Now the actual conversation starts. If your employee acknowledges the behavior, you can talk about how to improve. If your employee does not acknowledge it, you can give more examples. If that does not help either, you can suggest that your employee ask colleagues or friends if they have the same experience.

> For a while now, you have been irritated by an employee who has indicated that he is looking to get ahead in his career and make a promotion. The problem you have with him is not that he is ambitious, but that he does not back up his ambition with action. He regularly rejects assignments and asks you a lot of questions. As a result, you assign him fewer tasks than you would want. You wonder whether he can actually handle the responsibility. Here's how the talk could go (if you stick to the above steps):
>
> 'Hi Stijn, there's something I want to talk to you about. You told me that you want more responsibility. But at the same time, you come to me with questions about account X, and also about account Y (observation). This makes me think that you lack a clear idea as to how to solve problems yourself, which surprises me (thinking). I'm concerned about this (feeling). I've also noticed that I've become reluctant to assign you tasks (behavior). Can you see why? I'd like you to tell me what's going on (request).'

For many managers, this way of confronting employees with certain facts takes some getting used to. You may at first feel like a fish out of water as you follow the above steps, as following these confrontation steps will not exactly make your conversation more natural. Managers in my training courses have pointed out that it helps to prepare for a conversation by writing down the steps. At that point, you will probably not yet be aware of your feelings and what personal need of yours causes your irritation. It is then just a matter of doing it. The more your practice these steps, the more natural it will become.

Do you always need to act mature?

If your employee does not respond to your request or comes up with a counter-suggestion, you will probably get angry or disappointed, or take charge and impose your way. It is also difficult to stay calm when your employee, during the actual conversation, shows the exact behavior you are challenging your employee on. Do you then have to stay sympathetic the whole time?

That depends on what you want to get out of the conversation. If you want to make your employee come to work on time, just assume the macho role and say, 'These are the rules, this is how we do things here, so make sure you're on time from now on.' This is clear and honest. But since you are no longer equals in the conversation, chances are that your employee will indeed be on time (for a few weeks), out of a fear of sanctions. Your employee will be on time because that is what you want, not because your employee considers it important to be on time. This is fine sometimes, I am certainly not saying that you always have to be in mature mode. Still, if you want to find a solution together with your employee and engage as equals, the mature style and mature attitude will be the most effective.

Pitfalls

- Mother

Your mother instincts may keep you from challenging your employee on certain results or behavior. You may feel sorry for your employee, think your employee cannot handle it, or are confident that your employee has already realized that things are not going right. On top of that, you may be inclined to beat around the bush to go easy on your employee. So, although you do go and challenge your employee, you use only vague terms such as *proactive attitude*, *commercial acumen*, and *tactical communication*. When you do this, chances are your employee has no clue what exactly you are trying to say.

> When I was a manager myself, I often felt sorry for employees who weren't hitting their targets. I knew that they also felt bad about it, so I didn't want to make them feel worse. I didn't say anything about it, while some employees kept failing to hit their targets. I just didn't feel like policing them. But as a result, I wasn't taking the responsibility that came with my management role.

- Macho

Another possible pitfall is that you become overly critical or judgmental when calling employees to account. You may be impatient or very demanding, causing you to become critical very quickly. Or perhaps you have been in mole or mother mode for a while, feel tired and irritated, and therefore come out with a bad-tempered remark.

- Mole

A very common pitfall is that you avoid conversations that you should really be having, but which you dread. You will then often make excuses to yourself to get out of it, such as 'never mind, I'll point it out if it happens again' or 'who am I to call him out on this?' Or perhaps you hope that someone else will bring it up. Just think, do all your employees know exactly how you feel about their performance? We all duck a difficult conversation now and again.

Avoiding Pitfalls

Counter the urge to duck conversations and look for a mature way to confront respectfully. Approach your employee as your equal and as a competent person, so that you can call your employee to account in mature mode whenever performance is below par or behavior is inconsistent with what you agreed on. Repeating the mature mindset back to yourself (employees are responsible for their own task, job satisfaction, health, and they can take care of themselves) may help you be frank about what you think, see, and feel.

For the sake of equality in the conversation and to make sure that you both understand each other, you can ask your employee to repeat what you said back to you in his or her own words. This will also give you an idea of how your message has come across and whether you need to further explain yourself or add more information.

Macho
Angry → How dare you!
Belittling → Now, now
Correcting → That's no way to speak to me
Whataboutism → What about what you did the other day?

Mother
Comforting and downplaying → It's not that bad, is it?
Soothing → I get that you're having a hard time

Mole
Ignorance → I really don't get it
Victim → I just can't seem to get anything right
Challenging details → Yes, but that's not true, that's not how it went
Passive aggressive → You really wouldn't do that ever, right?
Emotional → Sad

What to Do: Be Mature
• Reflect on feelings → I can tell that you're surprised
• Explain → What I want to get across,...The reason why I'm telling you this is...
• Guess underlying need → I can imagine that you ...
• Express your need → I want to resolve this, work things out, strengthen ties
• Make a request or proposal → Let's talk it over and settle this

---

Figure 5.2   Responses to Feedback

Dealing with Responses

Respectful confrontation will trigger a response. In his or her response to you, your employee might also step into the mother, macho, or mole pitfall. In Figure 5.2, the three pitfalls are linked to typical responses or thoughts that go with these pitfalls. If you know your employees well, you may be able to anticipate how they will respond, which will, in turn, allow you to think about how you will respond back. This is what Figure 5.2 is all about, about how you can make sure that you stay out of the pitfalls and stay mature.

A macho response encapsulates a judgment. Your employee may, for example, reply that you are way out of line, slipping into the macho role and behaving angrily or with disdain. But your employee might also slip into the mother role, which would materialize in a caring response of trying to help you. Or your employee might go into mole mode, responding in a self-effacing and 'childish' way.

Whichever response you get, you will always need to take a step back and look at the situation objectively to prevent yourself from also becoming judgmental and to maintain the equality between you. Get into your helicopter and observe what is happening or what is about to happen between you and your employee. Once you have taken this breather, you can choose a mature response (see Figure 5.2).

I just talked to a member of my team about the fact that she missed several deadlines and keeps passing the buck to other departments. I told her that I've heard her say on several occasions that it is someone else's fault that she was unable to make a deadline. I noticed that I was getting irritated, so I got into the helicopter and tried to figure out what is going on. Is it me or is it her? What's happening? Even though I tried to be as mature as possible in what I said, my employee came back with a fairly angry response, saying that it's not true that she always blames others, but that she simply cannot do her job if the other department does not deliver what she needs. And she said that it's not her fault that other departments are falling short. 'She's doing it again!' I thought. Despite the strong temptation to get angry, I restrained myself because I wanted to stay effective in the conversation, and so I followed the steps and said, 'Judging by your response, you feel attacked by what I said (reflecting on feelings). I wanted to talk to you about this to explore ways to achieve better collaboration (explaining). It seems to me that you're rather annoyed with other departments and unable to do a good job as a result. Am I right? (guessing an underlying need) And I would like to sit down with you to see what you can do to improve the situation (my need). Shall we take a look at both these things?' (proposal)

- Are there any employees in your team you should really be confronting? And what should you confront them with?
- Is what you should challenge this employee about an incident, an accident, or a pattern? And might it also be of your own doing to a certain extent?
- Describe the steps of the conversation, what is your observation, the effect on you (thinking, feeling, and behavior). What is your request?
- How do you think your employee will respond?
- Describe how you could respond to an angry or submissive response from your employee.

The role of manager also involves assessing your employees' performance. Are they doing a good job, how are they doing compared to the expectations and compared to their peers?

Reviewing performance also includes imposing sanctions. Although it may sound negative, reviewing performance involves attaching consequences to your level of satisfaction or dissatisfaction with results and behavior. There is nothing more demotivating to employees than having poorly performing co-workers in the workplace who keep their jobs and even get a pay rise. Before going into a performance review with your employee, think about the consequences you want to attach to the employee's performance. Consequences can come in the form of rewards (if you complete this project successfully, you will be up for promotion) or sanctions (if you fail to improve your sales figures, you cannot continue in this job).

How Do You Do That?

The fact that you, as the manager, assess and penalize makes it hard to adopt a mature attitude in these kinds of talks, simply because assessing and penalizing someone clashes with the sense of equality you seek to convey in mature mode. Still, as the manager, you are never truly your employee's equal. There is no escaping that simple fact. After all, your employee will never be in a position to decide about your pay or contract, while you do have a say about theirs. You can try to infuse some level of equality into the performance review by being open to your employee's response and staying interested in how your employee assesses his or her own performance.

Giving Compliments

Reviewing performance and making adjustments also means to reward good behavior, such as by giving compliments. A compliment is positive acknowledgment of an effort, performance, or result. It is extremely important that you give compliments, because a compliment triggers the reward center in your employee's brain. A compliment reinforces your employee's self-image and forges a better relationship between the two of you. A compliment has an even greater motivational effect than a gift, a promotion, or money (provided the employee is happy with their salary). By regularly and openly giving compliments, you are stimulating a culture where people speak about each other in positive terms. If you make a habit of it, you will automatically see your perception of your employees change. It makes you more aware of positives, which will also do your own mood a lot of good.

Imagine you're giving a presentation to a group of co-workers. Halfway into the presentation, your laptop crashes, and it takes you a while to get it working again. The first critical question you get briefly throws you off. You struggle to find the right words and there are some giggles in the audience. You feel pretty unhappy about how the presentation went. When, the next day, your manager taps you on the shoulder and says, 'Well done yesterday,' how does that make you feel? What a dope. Was he not paying attention? Is he just trying to be nice? Or does he not get it at all?

Not quite the kind of thoughts the manager had hoped for when giving the compliment. What happened? Your thoughts are caused by the fact that it was not clear to you, as the recipient of the compliment, what your manager liked about the presentation. This is also how it works with your employees.

Go back to the example of the lousy presentation you gave, but now your manager says to you, 'Well done yesterday. I saw that, after your laptop crashed, you managed to keep presenting in a light-hearted manner, seemingly unfazed. And when you dealt with a very tricky question, you even managed to keep everyone focused and entertained by cracking a quick joke. I could tell that you had everything under control. I felt relaxed watching you present, and instantly knew that I can safely leave the upcoming presentations to you as well.'

What would you think now? Exactly! Hmm, he's got a point. I actually did a rather good job. And how perceptive of him.

When it comes to compliments, the following rules apply:
- Be generous with compliments: everybody needs positive reinforcement, compliments are always welcome. In fact, criticism weighs much more and lingers much longer than a compliment.
- Be honest and specific: just like with respectful confrontation, refer to specific behavior and the effect it had on you (thinking, feeling, behavior). Tell your employee what you appreciate about him or her and why.
- Don't delay compliments: do not save up your compliments until the performance review, or worse still, until your speech at your employee's retirement party.

Pitfalls
- Mother

When reviewing an employee's performance, you can also overdo it on the empathy ('I understand why you didn't make that deadline it, you were very busy'), which means that you are not entirely honest in your assessment. You may also slip into this role out of a kind of fear of undermining your employee's motivation through an honest assessment. You are then basically shielding your employee and not approaching him or her from a mature mindset.

- Macho

Perhaps you show too little empathy and are overly judgmental. When you notice that you are starting to tell your employees how to change, it means that you have stepped into the macho pitfall. In the macho role, you may also forget to give compliments. Due to the fact that you are irritated, you no longer see the things your employee does well.

- Mole

You might also slip into mole mode when doing performance reviews and keep your dissatisfaction to yourself. Or you might even opt out of doing performance reviews altogether.

Avoiding Pitfalls

Mature assessment means that you are open and honest about what you think and feel. It means that you prepare well for your employee's performance review and think about what you have seen and noticed over the past period. It means that you take stock of your employee's strengths and improvement needs. It means that you prepare the review in such a way that you have examples ready for all the points you intend to raise.

You do not pull your punches, because you realize that your employee will only have the opportunity to develop when he or she is aware of his or her strengths and improvement needs. You make it clear to your employee that you are bringing up these issues because you want to help your employee grow.

Performance Review

Many managers dread them, performance reviews. At most companies, there are clear arrangements in place as to what managers are expected to do in assessing employees' performance. Sometimes, there are even standard formats for the different kinds of talks (planning interview, performance review, evaluation interview). These formats will then list all the subjects to cover during the talk. At other companies, employees fill out a form themselves, or their manager will do it beforehand. The topics listed on the form are subsequently discussed. And yet, there are managers who do not take their performance review responsibility very seriously or who try to get out of it. With this in mind, I have formulated a number of tips on how to conduct a good performance review:

- Schedule the review well in advance. Take the appointment seriously, make enough time for it and do not reschedule.
- Ask your employee to prepare for the performance review. Also prepare for it yourself. Complete the assessment form beforehand. It will help if you make notes throughout the year. Ask yourself if you would hire this employee if he or she were applying for this position now. And if you would have liked a different type or an employee with different skills, what does that say about your employee's development needs?
- Create a relaxed atmosphere during the performance review. Your employee may be nervous. Make sure your employee feels at ease. Take your time, choose a quiet spot. Break the ice with a light-hearted subject or a joke. Ask your employee whether he or she feels tense. Not sitting directly opposite each other will help create a relaxed atmosphere.
- To be able to assess whether certain goals have been achieved, set SMART goals during the planning interview at the start of the year. These results are not visible and need assessing. Also draw on reports from previous meetings, planning interviews, and performance reviews.
- First talk about what you think your employee is doing well. Give genuine compliments about good results or behavior you appreciate in your employee. Make your employee aware of the impact of his or her behavior.
- Then go into the development needs. Remember to stay in mature mode. Do not judge but share what you have seen and what you think from a position of equals. You could even prepare for this by using the steps of respectful confrontation (Figure 5.1). Do not focus only on achieving results, but also on your employee's work ethic and behavior.
- If relevant, you could even refer to other people's opinion in your assessment. You could get your employee to ask for a second opinion from co-workers, customers, or direct reports.
- A negative review must never come as a surprise. Make sure that possible development needs have been discussed on several previous occasions, in performance reviews, evaluation interviews and during regular meetings. Never wait until the formal review to bring up development needs for the first time.
- And last but not least, even though you are assessing your employee's performance, do listen to your employee's feedback on your assessment. In fact, ask your employee for feedback. And use your employee's take on the review to improve your own performance as a manager or the performance of the company as a whole.

> Imagine you were to do performance reviews now. In a few words, what would your assessment of each of your employees' performance be? Split your assessment up into three parts:
> - Overall assessment
> - Strengths (which can be developed further)
> - Development needs for the employee to work on
>
> Try to think of a compliment to give each employee.
> What could you do over the coming period to make sure these assessments will not come as a complete surprise to your employees?

Delivering Bad News

Another conversation technique you are going to need in a leadership position is the technique for delivering bad news, because that simply needs to be done sometimes. The difference compared to respectful confrontation is that a bad-news talk departs from a fixed message you need to get across. Such a fixed message could be that you will not be renewing your employee's contract, or your employee will not get the pay rise/promotion/major project he or she had hoped for.

Before You Begin

An important given is that a bad-news talk often ends with your employee feeling bad. There is basically no escaping this. The reason I am stating this so explicitly is that most managers quietly hope for a happy ending, thus stepping into the mother pitfall. But the fact of the matter is that when you deny your employee a pay rise, or do not renew your employee's contract, chances are that your employee will be disappointed, or even angry. Just try to accept that. It helps to realize that you cannot prevent your employee from feeling lousy. What you can do, however, is try to be as meticulous as possible in conducting the conversation. In the following, I will go into how this is done.

It is always a good idea to prepare well for these kinds of conversations. What exactly are you going to say? What is the reasoning you're going to use? What response from your employee do you expect to get? And how do you feel about the whole thing? Do you feel guilty? Uneasy? Irritated? Also make sure there is sufficient time for the talk and have it in a room where you can have privacy.

The Talk Itself

What is the best way to deliver bad news? Figure 5.3 illustrates the three steps of a bad-news talk.

1. Delivering the Blow

Deliver the bad news right away, without holding back. Possible pitfalls are that you start beating around the bush or first ask how your employee's weekend was. Don't do that. Deliver the news right away and be clear. Get straight to the point by saying something along the lines of, 'Jorick, I'm going to come straight out with it. I've got some bad news for you. We will not be renewing your contract.' Do not try to sugarcoat the message or soften the blow through cautious formulation, as that could create the risk of your employee not understanding what you are saying. Next, give one or two clear reasons for the decision. Do not overdo it on the reasons, because that would detract from the core of your message or could lead you into a discussion.

Pitfall: Make sure you do not use the questioning technique of giving your employee 'rope to hang himself or herself with,' which is when you try to get your employee to say what you are thinking but are afraid to say. This basically consists in asking your employee leading questions to get your employee to say what you are afraid to say but are thinking. When you ask, 'Jorick, do you personally think things have been going well recently?' you are leading your employee to your way of thinking in very subtle way.

2. Managing the Reaction

Give your employee some space to get over the initial shock. This step is the hardest, it will feel like it drags on for hours, but that is because you will probably feel awkward. The bad news can trigger different reactions, ranging from disbelief, denial, anger, acceptance, and indifference to relief and a counter-attack. At this stage of the talk, try to only be understanding in your response to your employee's reaction, acknowledge your employee's reaction. Say things like, 'I can understand you're shocked,' 'I can see that you're angry,' or 'I can hear in your voice that you're disappointed.' Accept what your employee says, without going into what your employee says. It is not about agreeing or disagreeing with your employee, it is purely about showing understanding of what your employee thinks and feels.

Perhaps your employee will go on the counter-attack and say things like, 'But last week when we all went for drinks after work, we had such a nice conversation.' If so, try not to react, because that will only lead you into a whole other conversation. Simply be understanding and tie in with what your employee says, which you do by listening with empathy, by uh-huhing and nodding, and by recapping your employee's words, as in, 'So you didn't see this coming at all?'

Aside from the employee's words, you can also recap your employee's feelings. This means that you repeat not only what your employee said, but also the feeling that went with it. This can be extremely hard to do, because you may not entirely agree with what your employee says or thinks.

Pitfall: a pitfall is that you go into macho mode and say something like, 'Surely this can't come as a surprise to you, we must have talked about this a dozen times!' Another pitfall is you wanting to make it all better for the other (mother role). That is when you start looking for the silver lining by saying, for example, 'See it as new opportunity' or 'Didn't you once say you always wanted to work at a smaller firm?' But remember, it is not your job to fix things and you are not the right person to comfort your employee.

As a basic rule, allow silences and give your employee the time to get over the shock and experience the feeling triggered by the news. Bite your tongue when your employee momentarily falls silent. To your employee, your message is truly bad news. During a moment of silence, your employee may be going over the consequences in his or her head, thinking about how to tell friends the news, how to proceed in life etc. Give your employee some time and suppress the urge to start justifying yourself by explaining that you had no choice. At training sessions for managers, we often practice these kinds of talks, and this step is the one that requires the most practice and patience. Participants in my training sessions soon realize that it is really all about leaning back and not filling the silences, but just letting them be.

3. *Solution, Explanation, Follow-Up Appointment*

After a while, your employee will have gotten over the initial shock and may feel less upset. The disappointment starts to fade. You can see it in your employee's attitude or in the fact that your employee comes to you with a 'why' or 'what now' question. This is an opportunity for you to check whether your employee has understood your explanation and reasoning. Sometimes it makes sense at this stage to reiterate your reasons, because your employee may not have taken it all in due to the shock. Try to use the same words every time you explain your reasons, otherwise things may get incoherent for your employee and you may end up in a discussion about details.

What works best is to ask your employee whether he or she is ready to talk about how to proceed. If so, you can go over the follow-up steps, but you can also suggest coming back to this later. Again, be mindful of what your employee can handle. And try to adapt to your employee's pace.

Bad news
1. Delivering the Blow
2. Managing the Reaction
3. Solution | Explanation | Follow-Up Appointment

The most common pitfalls of each step:

1. **Delivering the blow**
   · Postponing the bad news
   · Sugarcoating the message | Beating around the bush
   · 'Hang yourself' method
   · Apologizing in advance

2. **Managing the reaction**
   · Not taking enough time
   · Silver lining
   · Justifying yourself
   · Filling the silences

3. **Solution | Explanation | Follow-Up Appointment**
   · Giving the employee too little space

Figure 5.3   Respectful Confrontation

- If you had to deliver bad news, how do you think your employee would react?
- Describe what you would say at step 1.

5.4 Summary

When performing the tasks that go with your manager role, you are bound to encounter pitfalls. If you stay in mature mode, you will prevent yourself from falling into them. Tasks of the manager:

1. *Translates vision to goals*
Pitfall: you put it off or are not clear about the goals, because you want to be liked. Or the goals are overly ambitious, causing your employee to become demotivated.

Mature: you set achievable goals.

2. *Monitors and reviews results and behavior*

Pitfall: you use vague language. Mole – you do not call your employee to account, even though you should. Mother – you do not call your employee to account on something because you pity your employee. Macho – you are overly critical or too judgmental when calling an employee to account on something.

Mature: you are honest and clear in what you think and feel. You see your employee as a sensible and competent person. During conversations, you ask your employee to recap what you discussed.

If things are not going the way you want, you can talk to your employee about that by confronting your employee respectfully. This means that you challenge your employee on the behavior that is bothering you or that is stifling your employee's development. First explore, however, whether your dissatisfaction is your own doing. If it is not, have the talk by following these steps: 1. Identify the behavior; 2. Explain what effect it is having on you (on your thinking, feelings, and behavior). Check whether your employee recognizes or understands what you are saying; 3. Make a request.

Your employee may subsequently get angry or challenge you (macho), be concerned (mother), or self-efface and react childishly (mole). Be prepared for all of that. Briefly get into your helicopter and then select a mature response, a response that adheres to the rules of feedback. Say what you feel, what your intention was, be frank about what you think your employee needs, and say what you would like to see happen next.

3. *Assesses and makes adjustments*

Pitfalls: Mole – you do not say to your employee that you are unhappy with his or her performance. Mother – you are too sympathetic. Macho – you feel little empathy, are critical and judgmental, or you never give compliments.

Mature: say what you have to say, as equals. Be generous with compliments and be genuine and specific in your compliments.

When having a performance review, make sure you prepare for it. First talk about what is going well, and then move on to the development needs. A negative review must never come as a surprise. Also listen to your employee's opinion and ideas.

As a manager, you are bound to have to deliver bad news now and again. Again, preparation is everything. Deliver the bad news right away and in no uncertain terms, and then manage the reaction. Take time for this and do not feel compelled to fill the silences that will inevitably occur. And then ask whether your employee is up to discussing how to proceed or would prefer to do that later.

6　Coach

This chapter is about the coaching mindset, about how, in a leadership position, to lean back like a coach and get your employees to take responsibility for their problems, tasks, and job satisfaction.

In the roles of leader and manager, you take responsibility for goal setting and performance assessment, but in the coach role, you pass that responsibility on to your employee. Not until you adopt the mature mindset as your personal belief (everyone is responsible for their own problems) will you be able to help your employees grow. A good coach helps the person they coach (the coachee) make their own steps toward their own chosen goal. The coach does not make the coachee dependent on him or her. The coach does not give tips or advice but trusts the other to be able to make their own choices in pursuing personal development. This approach is the one to use when switching to coaching mode.

But the question is when to make this switch. TheAnswer is when your employee has something on his or her mind. When your employee comes to you with a problem or a question, you can use a coaching attitude to give your employee the strength to be able to come up with solutions. And you can deploy coaching techniques when your employee wants to pursue personal and professional development.

At most companies, employees have performance reviews at least once a year. During these reviews, manager and employee go over the employee's development targets. I strongly advise you to discuss development more often than once a year. If you value development, make some time once a month to discuss your employee's development needs and progress.

> **The Added Difficulty of Coaching**
> For you as a manager, it is harder to switch to a coaching role than it is for an external coach. Knowing your employee well is actually a handicap, as it will make you more inclined to go into mother mode (I'll help you) or macho mode (I know what's best). It is harder to

stay curious if you already know a lot or have a firm opinion about something. And from your leadership position, you generally have fixed ideas as to how your employees should do their jobs. You already have an opinion, negative or positive, on their behavior and performance. Switching from the

manager role (where you assess and adjust their performance) to the coach role (where you coach your employees in their development) can be tricky. When an employee wants to develop in a certain direction and you had an entirely different direction in mind, for example, you will struggle to go into coaching mode and support this employee. In that case, you have no other option than to abandon the coach role and go back into leader and manager mode to tell this employee about your strategy and what you expect this employee to do.

6.1   Coach: Encourages Others to Find Their Own Solutions

What exactly does a coach do? Coaches do not give tips and advice (although many believe otherwise), but instead they make sure their coachees take responsibility for examining and solving their own 'problems.' If you want to switch from leader or manager mode to coach mode, you need a coaching mindset. By coaching mindset, I mean that you approach your employee in a mature way, from a belief that your employee is personally responsible for his or her performance, health, and job satisfaction. You can approach your employee with empathy and warmth, albeit without slipping into the mother role. There is no need to help or rescue your employee. If your employee is insecure, for example, it is not up to you to restore your employee's self-confidence, you should be able to accept the insecurity and let your employee decide what to do about it. And it means that you are not judging the insecurity, like a macho would do, not telling your employee what to do or what the goal should be. That is unless the insecurity causes you problems or you can tell that it affects your employee's performance, because then you would have to engage in respectful confrontation.

How Do You Do That?

A good coach is not just someone who is warm and not judgmental. A good coach can also confront and be open, honest, and clear. When approaching an employee from a coaching mindset, you are warm and empathic, but also open and honest. The main thing is that you place ultimate responsibility in your employee's hands. Your employee is responsible for his or her personal development, not you. Your employee has to do the work, not you. You can lean back and ask questions that will help your employee gain awareness, give your employee self-confidence, and help your employee take steps toward a specific goal. The coaching mindset will help you get the other to come up with solutions. You are the facilitator, but you actually do not do all that much.

> One of my employees came to me saying that she doesn't really like her job anymore. She has been responsible for the same project for a few years now, and she's doing a good job, but I do understand that she hasn't really been challenged for a while. In a reflex, I made a few suggestions as to how she could make her job fun again. I passed one of my projects on to her and suggested that she help out a colleague who I know is overworked. And I showed her how to make her project a bit more challenging by working together with new partners.
>
> Oops. I was doing all the work for her. I was solving her problems for her. She'll probably be back in my office next week telling me that she doesn't like my project at all. I let my mother and macho reflexes take over. The mother approach emerged when I tried to help her, coming up with several possible solutions. And I also slipped into the macho role when I told her that she could make her project more challenging herself.
>
> *Question:* How could I have been more of a coach in this situation?
>
> *Answer:* If I had approached this matter from the mature mindset, I would not have considered it up to me to improve my employee's job satisfaction, but I would have left it in her own hands. From a mature mindset, I would have been able to ask coaching questions. 'So, your work is not challenging enough for you anymore. What do you intend to do about it? What could you do to change it? What do you want from me?' It would then have been up to my employee to explore her options herself and think about what she needs to enjoy her job more. It would have been be up to her to indicate what kind of projects or tasks she would prefer and to formulate a clear question to me. That is when she would be doing the work, and not I.

Showing Empathy

An important aspect of the coaching mindset is that you show empathy. Empathy is the ability to put yourself in someone else's shoes and relate to their thinking and experiences. Showing empathy is an essential requirement when you want to coach your employee. After all, your employee needs to feel safe with you and be able to be open and honest with you. Only in such a safe environment will you be able to help your employee track down the causes of and solutions to their problems.

Empathy does not only mean that you understand your employee and are able to assume your employee's perspective, it also means that you are able to accept without judging the fact that your employee is angry, upset, or frustrated. It may perhaps sound woolly, but it is about 'letting it be' and not giving in to the urge to cure or fix it. More often than not, we immediately step into pitfalls when confronted with someone who feels bad, wanting to resolve it right away. Imagine that someone from your team told you that she was so stressed that she was having trouble sleeping. What would you say?

- 'You shouldn't check your email late at night.'
- 'Ah well, we're all busy.'
- 'As soon as the website is live, it will all quieten down.'

They sound empathetic and nice, these uplifting responses, don't they? But truly empathetic they are not. Sure, the intention behind them is good, trying to make the other feel better, but they do not show empathy. This is because all these reactions imply that your employee should not feel that way, that there is no need to be stressed. The mother role took over, because you felt that you had to fix the stress. When you take a mature approach to an employee who feels bad, you realize that it is not your responsibility, but your employee's own responsibility to find ways to feel better. Of course, it is very unfortunate for your employee that he or she feels that way, but you also believe that your employee can handle it. It is not up to you to resolve it.

Pitfalls

I have made a list of pitfalls, a list of things to avoid when you want to show empathy in your response to an angry, upset, scared, or insecure employee.

- Comparing and going one worse: to tell a story that is even worse ('It happened to me once as well, but my project was even bigger'). This is sometimes referred to as autobiographical listening, where you relate everything the other says to yourself.
- Educating and giving advice: to say that you know what the solution to your employee's problem is ('Here's what you should do...').
- Playing down the problem, or pointing out the silver lining: by this I mean trying to take the sting out of the problem by drawing a silver lining around that dark cloud ('OK, you're having a hard time now, but you'll learn from it' or 'Try to see the positive side, if you can ultimately handle this project, you can handle anything.').
- Interrogating: this is not the same as to ask further questions. To interrogate is to be like a detective and ask questions that are not entirely relevant and only steer the other away from their feelings ('How exactly did it go, when exactly was that?').
- Seeking understanding for the other side: 'Try putting yourself in his shoes' or 'He's probably very busy and that's why he's so blunt.'

- Analyzing/psychoanalyzing: 'Yes, I think your insecurity stems from your childhood.'
- Joining in and making it worse: 'Oh, how awful for you and you were also sick this year, weren't you?'

As you read these coaching don'ts, you may think to yourself, 'I do this sometimes, but my intentions are good' or 'It does work when trying to make the other feel better.' I get that, because I have stepped into these pitfalls myself. That you mean well is undeniable, of course, but meaning well will not automatically lead to the other accepting their feelings. And you need that acceptance to be able to make your employee take ownership of these feelings. Plus, it can be plain exhausting to try to make your employee feel better. So, now we know what pitfalls to watch out for, it is time for a few tips on how to get it right, how to show empathy.

Avoiding Pitfalls

What you can do to give the other some space and let their feelings exist is to

- Truly listen: this one is obvious and all about being genuinely open to what your employee has to say.
- Recap: to recap your employee's words, as well as the feelings and emotions your employee expresses or that you picked up on in your employee's demeanor
- Ask further questions, encourage: ask open-ended questions to get your employee to tell you more.
- Show understanding: communicate that you understand what your employee is saying.
- Mirror: reflect your employee's behavior back to him or her
- Guess feelings and needs: guess what you think your employee feels or what your employee needs ('It seems to me that you are very annoyed about that' or 'I think what you want is to feel more appreciated').
- Support: let your employee know that you stand by him or her and are not judging your employee or the situation; you can also let your employee know that you feel bad for him or her.
- Look for ways to connect to it: if the situation is not one you recognize from your own personal experience, look for aspects that you can relate to. This could be when you, for example, do not quite understand why your employee is anxious about an upcoming important phone call, because you never get anxious about phone calls. When this happens, you can ask yourself what part of this anxiety you can relate to. When do you feel anxious about something you have to do? You can then tap into that feeling and try to understand your employee, even though you do not recognize the actual situation.

When it comes to showing empathy, less is more. Giving someone space to feel bad is mostly a question of doing nothing or doing very little. You can then just say something along the lines of, 'Gosh' or 'That's terrible' and then stay silent to give your employee space to really feel what he or she feels. The next step in the interaction will then be initiated by your employee, as soon as your employee is ready. At first, you may feel ill at ease or even unkind when you limit your response like this and refrain from trying to fix the situation, but just try it and see what happens!

Tip: go online and watch Brené Brown's *Empathy vs sympathy* video. This short animation explains what empathy is and how we tend to react. I have borrowed the concept of silver lining from this video.

> - Are there any employees with whom you have trouble showing empathy?
> - Knowing this, what could you do next time to respond with greater empathy to this employee?

Walk-Ins

A coaching mindset will also come in handy when dealing with walk-ins. 'Do you have a minute?' 'Can I ask you something?' It probably sounds familiar. You are trying to get some work done, and suddenly one of your employees walks into your office. When I was a manager, I was interrupted by employees at least twenty times every day. Some had a question, some needed me to sign off on something, but often they just needed to get something off their chest, and even more often it was not even clear to me what they wanted from me, but I would still say, 'Come in, take a seat!' I wanted to be there for them and help them with their problems and questions (yes, I know, very motherly).

For the sake of convenience, I will refer to them as 'walk-ins.' Most managers will recognize this. There are physical walk-ins, but also callers, texters, and emailers.

Needless to say, some of these walk-ins do actually raise urgent matters that you want to deal with right away. If your employee is truly having a crisis, either at work or at home, you want to be there for this employee. And there are also walk-ins who come to you with a clear question or idea, such as:

- Can you sign off on this for me?
- Will you be in the office this afternoon?
- I can do Sam's meeting for him, just so you know.
- I have an idea to boost sales, can I run it by you?

These are walk-ins you can deal with quickly or thank for their input. The walk-ins that bothered me were the ones that came to me without a clear question or need. Walk-ins who came in with a vague problem, with a hugely elaborate story. How do you prevent wasting hours on those kinds of walk-ins? How do you make sure you do not take responsibility and start fixing everyone's problems? This is what Figure 6.1 is all about.

Switch Your Walk-In to Active Mode

First of all, it helps to approach walk-ins from a mature mindset. If you manage that, you are relying on your employee to come up with solutions to his or her problems. When adopting this mindset in your response to walk-ins, the first thing you do is figure out what the employee actually wants from you. Then you can decide what to do with that request. Are you going to go into it? Are you going toAnswer the question? Or are you going to look for the 'why' behind your employee's question? Whatever you choose to do, it will not consist in producing solutions out of a reflex, but instead in acting based on a conscious choice.

Your employee walks in all upset, making a lot of noise. She goes on about an argument she just had with a co-worker at the accounts department. You begin by respectfully interrupting her, calling her by her name and saying, 'Forgive me for interrupting.' Next, you take her perspective and mirror her feelings by saying that you can see her emotion, saying, 'I can see you're upset.' And then you ask the big question, 'What's your question?' You can frame this question differently by saying, for example, 'For me to be able to help, I'd like to know what you're asking me to do.'

This way, you are placing responsibility for the problem with her. She will then think briefly and say that she doesn't actually need anything from you, but just wanted to get it off her chest. Or she might now ask for a solution to her problem. Or she could want you to back her. Whatever she asks, it is now up to you to decide whether or not you are going to give her what she asks. This is when you commit to doing or not doing something. So, depending on your diary and your time, you decide whether you want to take the time now or later to listen to what she has to say. You could say, for example, 'I've only got five minutes, if you come back after my MT meeting, I've got half an hour for you.'

Getting Used to It

Personally, it took me a while to get used to this approach. It initially felt to me as if I was being rude by not inviting my employee in and not switching into help mode. But I ultimately found that I got a lot out of this approach, despite the uneasy feeling. More than anything, it saved me a lot of time. And employees also got used to it and started walking into my office less.

1. Respectful interruption

2. Emotion reflection
   '*I can see that it's affecting you a lot*'
   '*I understand that you want to speak to me now*'

3. What do you want from me? What's your question?

4. Commit: on a certain condition, now, later, or not at all

↓

If an employee keeps walking in: give feedback on their pattern

Figure 6.1   Walk-Ins

As you can see in Figure 6.1, an employee may still continue to keep walking into your office. If so, it has become a pattern, repeated behavior, and you should give feedback on this pattern. Use the steps of respectful confrontation to make your employee aware of the fact that he or she is a regular walk-in, what effect this constant walking in is having on you, and what you would like your employee to do instead.

- What kinds of questions or problems do your walk-ins tend to have?
- How will you respond to your walk-ins over the coming days?
- Do you also have regular walk-ins who you should actually confront with the fact that they come and see you far too often?

6.2   Coach: Facilitates the Development of Others (Who Are Not Aware of the Coaching Need)

Coaching sessions should primarily be geared toward an employee's coaching need. In my role of coach, I almost always get to coach people who have a specific coaching need, a coaching goal. People turn to coaching to, for example, become more assertive or better at handling stress. But when you, from your leadership position, want to start coaching, you sometimes find that your employee does not even have a coaching goal, or is not aware of his or her coaching goal. You know that your employee needs to change, but your employee does not know it (yet).

How Do You Do That?

There is no coaching without a coaching need. This is a crucial given. If your employee does not have a goal or cannot think of one, asking your employee coaching questions is pointless. Coaching is possible only if your employee wants to be coached. After all, if you start coaching and your employee is not open to it, you are the one doing all the work. And coaching is about you putting your employee to work, getting your employee to start analyzing, exploring, and troubleshooting.

But how do you get started when you see a coaching goal, but your employee does not? Well, that is where Figure 6.2 comes in.

Pitfall

Some managers have a tendency to, as soon as they see a development need in an employee, switch to coaching mode right away. They start asking questions to activate the employee, questions such as, 'What could you do to raise your profile?' But the problem is that the employee does not even know yet that change is needed and why. And changing is hard enough as it is. To be able to change, your goal needs to be attractive and urgent. And the goal needs to be your own, not someone else's. So, when you try to coach your employee without your employee being aware of or committed to it, chances of success are slim. And it will be extremely tiresome, because you are basically flogging a dead horse.

> One of your employees tends to stay quiet at meetings. He stares aimlessly and doodles in his notebook, and he doesn't say anything, not even when the discussion moves on to his area of responsibility. You notice that his co-workers are clueless as to what he thinks and does. He is somewhat invisible. You feel that he should make his presence felt, because no one takes him seriously this way.

Avoiding the Pitfall

What can you do to make sure that the goal you have in mind also becomes your employee's goal?

Respectful Confrontation

The first step is respectful confrontation. Communicating what you have seen and what you would want to see. Your employee first needs to know what specific behavioral aspect you want your employee to change. When you confront respectfully, you address your employee in a mature way, without being judgmental (macho) or overly caring (mother). You communicate what effect your employee's behavior is having on you, and what you would want, as specified in Section 5.2.

As soon as you have confronted, you can expect one of several reactions:

• Yes, I want to change

The ideal reaction is when your employee says, 'Yes, I recognize that, I want to do something about it.' This means you can get started, you can offer to work on it together. You can even decide to start right away or schedule a coaching session and coach your employee on this subject. How to do this is explained in Section 6.3.

Your employee may also say 'yes' but exude 'no,' which feels like a false 'yes'. You can then sense that your employee only agrees to go along with the coaching to please you or to put an end to the conversation. When this happens, you have two options. You can start a coaching session on your employee's change goal and see whether it leads anywhere (perhaps your employee is more motivated than you thought) or you can confront your employee with his or her non-verbal resistance. You could say, 'You say you want to change, but I can see you're not sure. What's that all about?'

• Huh, I've never been told that before

The fact is that we do not live in an ideal world. It may very well be that your employee does not recognize your feedback, that it really is the first time this development need has ever been raised or that your employee is even somewhat taken aback by it. If so, give your employee some space to digest it. You could ask your employee to take charge of the any-other-business part of the meeting and to ask co-workers or friends for feedback. This would automatically trigger a response of 'Yes, I want to change' or 'No, I don't think I need to change.'

• No, I don't think I need to change (This is just the way I am)

Your employee may not see the need to change or throw cold water on all your good intentions by saying, 'This is just the way I am,' which is a firm 'no'. No, I don't want to change. Still, it could also be that your employee wants to change but is afraid to. Changing can be quite a challenge. There can be all kinds of emotions hidden behind your employee's rotund 'no'. But what is the most important thing at this point is for you to be aware of that fact that your employee does not want to change (yet), meaning that you know that now is not the time to start coaching. But what can you do?

Carrot or Stick

When you get a 'no' or a lukewarm response, you can resort to using a 'carrot' or a 'stick'. The carrot is an incentive you hold out to your employee, as you try to tempt your employee by showing what he or she stands to gain from changing: 'Wouldn't it be great if more people were able to rely on you for the things you're good at?' 'Wouldn't it be nice if more people were to listen to you?' 'How great would it be if you were less stressed?' This is you trying to make the change sound attractive.

The alternative approach is the 'stick,' an entirely different way of activating your employee. Instead of emphasizing the benefits, you point out the consequences of not changing, in an attempt to put some urgency behind the change. This is when you say things like, 'If you don't step up your game at meetings, you will not get a promotion' or 'If you don't start communicating more clearly, you will not get a good score on your performance review' or 'If you don't forge a better working relationship with department X, you will miss out on new projects.'

The carrot and the stick can both be effective. Some managers are more inclined to dangle the carrot, while others prefer to wield the stick. You could even use them both, one after the other. They both help you motivate your employee to change.

Still Unsuccessful

If the positive or negative prospect offered by the carrot or the stick actually goads your employee into deciding to change, you can start coaching. But if you still do not have a firm 'yes' from your employee, there are three further options:

- Change: think of a trick, something wacky, something you haven't tried yet, whatever, anything.
- Accept: accept that the other will not change. Only you can decide if that is acceptable or not. In some cases, your employee's development goal is essential for continued performance, while in other cases it is merely a plus.
- Execute the consequences from the stick approach, which means no promotion, no big project, or no new contract for your employee.

The key is to not start coaching, or trying to coach, an employee who does not want to be coached. What I personally used to do was try to use leading questions to activate someone. 'Don't you want a higher profile for yourself?' Or I started helping or coaching without the other knowing exactly what I wanted to achieve. As you will know by now, this never works, because it means you are doing all the work (mother). It is not mature, and so it will only be an energy drain for you.

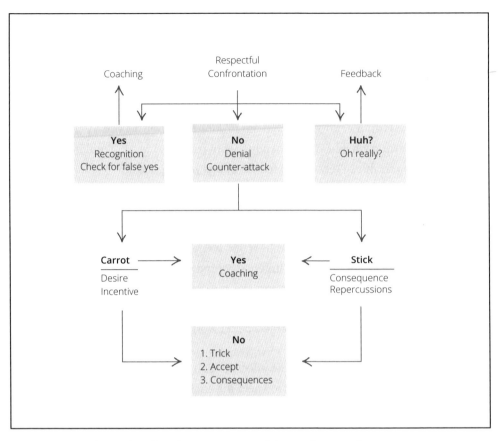

Figure 6.2   Coaching when the other is not aware of the coaching need

- For each of your employees, define the main learning goal.
- Did you confront respectfully? And were you clear about that or were you overly cautious? Have you tried using the 'carrot' or the 'stick'?
- If your employee fails or refuses to change, will that be too bad or unacceptable?

6.3   Coach: Facilitates the Development of Others (Who Are Aware of the Coaching Need)

As I already explained, you need to be careful not to start coaching when your employee is not committed to changing, you're essentially flogging a dead horse and wasting your energy.

How Do You Do That?

If you have managed to convince your employee of the need to change, you can start coaching. But it can, of course, also be that your employee came to you asking for help and was already aware of the need to change. Or perhaps your employee says during a performance review that he or she would like to change. Regardless of how you got here, you are dealing with an employee who wants to change and has solicited your help in doing so, and so you can start coaching. But how?

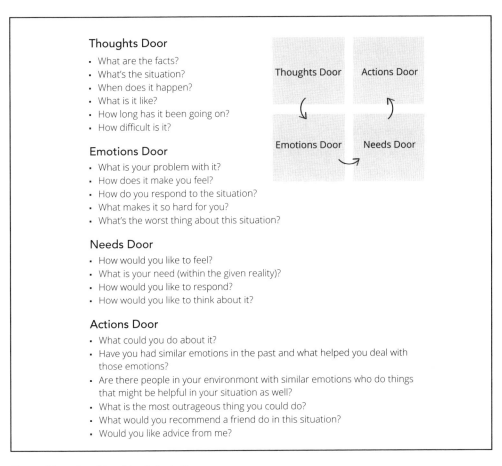

Thoughts Door

- What are the facts?
- What's the situation?
- When does it happen?
- What is it like?
- How long has it been going on?
- How difficult is it?

Emotions Door

- What is your problem with it?
- How does it make you feel?
- How do you respond to the situation?
- What makes it so hard for you?
- What's the worst thing about this situation?

Needs Door

- How would you like to feel?
- What is your need (within the given reality)?
- How would you like to respond?
- How would you like to think about it?

Actions Door

- What could you do about it?
- Have you had similar emotions in the past and what helped you deal with those emotions?
- Are there people in your environmont with similar emotions who do things that might be helpful in your situation as well?
- What is the most outrageous thing you could do?
- What would you recommend a friend do in this situation?
- Would you like advice from me?

Figure 6.3   Coaching Matrix in Action

The Coaching Matrix

There are different structures and tools you can use for coaching sessions. One useful tool in activating employees is the coaching matrix. This technique designed by Maarten Kouwenhoven (2007) enables you to analyze the situation that is bothering your employee and get your employee to come up with solutions to the problem.

The coaching matrix is made up of four quadrants that are called 'doors,' because you have to go through them to get to the next stage: a thoughts door, an emotions door, a needs door, and an actions door. As you can see in Figure 6.3, it begins with the thoughts door. This is where you ask your employee to share his or her thoughts on the situation, as you want to get an idea of the facts and the context. Typical thoughts door questions include the following:

- What are the facts?
- What's the situation?
- When does it happen?
- What is it like?
- How long has it been going on?
- How difficult is it?

There is no need to ask all these questions, simply select the ones that are appropriate for your employee's problem.

Next, you could ask, 'And what are your feelings with that?' or 'What is your problem with that?' These questions open the emotions door. I sometimes notice that managers are reluctant to go through the emotions door and ask employees about their feelings, because they feel that it then all becomes too fuzzy or soft and that facts have greater relevance. But it is important that you know what exactly is causing the employee to consider the situation problematic. And you will often only be able to get to that understanding by discussing emotions. So, by all means, ask your employee about his or her emotions. The following questions will open the emotions door:

- What's the worst thing about this situation?
- How do you respond to the situation?
- What makes it so hard for you?

If your employee struggles to communicate emotions and you notice that your employee is still sharing thoughts, you can point out that there are four basic emotions, namely fear, anger, happiness, and sadness, and that every emotion a person can have will be related to one of these basic emotions. Frustration and irritation, for example, are forms of anger, while concerns and tension are forms of fear.

After your employee has communicated emotions, you can proceed to the needs door by asking questions such as the following:

- How would you like to feel?
- What is your need (within the given reality)?
- How would you like to respond?
- How would you like to think about it?

This stage of the session will often produce an outcome that is the positive opposite of what your employee said during the emotions stage. If your employee, for example, says that others need to change, saying things like, 'I want things to change' or 'I want others to listen to me,' explain that it is not possible to change the situation or the other, but that it is possible to change how your employee approaches or deals with it. Ask your employee to put into words what he or she needs in the given reality. Once your employee's needs have been formulated, shift the conversation to the actions door by asking questions such as:

- What could you do?
- Have you had similar emotions in the past and what helped you deal with those emotions?
- Are there people in your environment with similar emotions who do things that might be helpful in your situation as well?
- What is the most outrageous thing you could do?
- What would you recommend a friend do in this situation?
- Would you like advice from me?

This final step of coming up with solutions wraps up the four-door round of questioning. Give your employee some space to come up with solutions without your help. Stay out of the mother role (of giving suggestions) or macho role (of rejecting your employee's own solutions and prodding your employee into a certain direction by saying things such as, 'Good idea' or 'Do you really think that'll work?') This latter part is not easy, I realize that, especially when you personally have all kinds ideas about the solutions your employee produces. But if you want your employee to take ownership of his or her change, now is the time to bite your tongue and let your employee go it alone.

What I love about this compact coaching technique is its simplicity and clarity, and that your employee can keep applying it after having gone through it with you several times. You will find that everyone has a different preferred door. Some people only go on about facts (thoughts door), while others dwell on feelings (emotions door). You probably have a preference yourself as well. Therefore, when trying to coach an employee who struggles to communicate emotions, and you are not very touchy-feely yourself either, it will be you who has to make an extra effort to still address emotions.

Pitfall

The most common coaching pitfall is the tendency to give advice or tell the coachee what you would do. This is not coaching or mature, because giving advice is basically telling the coachee that he or she is incapable of solving the problem without your help. It is you making your employee smaller, and more dependent on you.

Another pitfall is rushing it. A coaching session takes some time, and patience. After all, it is an occasion for your employee to explore feelings and to try to find solutions to get closer to a certain goal. This is not something you can do in a few minutes.

And the final pitfall I want to highlight is your potential tendency to work hard, to look for patterns, to produce solutions, and to analyze the problem. The idea of a coaching session is to have your employee do all the hard work. It is your employee who needs to sit up straight and be alert, to rack his or her brain trying toAnswer your coaching questions, and to find connections and possible solutions.

Avoiding the Pitfall

To stay in coaching mode, recall the beliefs that underpin mature leadership. Your employee is personally responsible and competent! Coaching is to trust the other to understand the problem and know what to do about it. And to also let that trust shine through in your questions and attitude, as you exude the confidence that your employee knows what the problem is and how to solve it.

In real life, this means biting your tongue a lot, I know this from personal experience. So, keep your sage advice to yourself, let silences be, and do not interfere with the solutions your employee comes up with. It is all about doing more by doing less.

Helpful Coaching Tools

The Scale Question

A practical coaching tool you can use is the scale question (see Figure 6.4). Use this tool when you have agreed on what your employee wants work on. If your employee does not yet have a clear idea as to what to develop, or you are not sure whether you and your employee are on the same page, you can ask your employee what the ideal situation looks like. What does your employee want to have more of or be able to do more of? Ask your employee to formulate in positive terms. So, instead of, 'I think I've lost the ability to give good presentations,' you want your employee to say, 'I'm confident that I can do good presentations.'

If your employee is able to identify the goal, draw a scale on a piece of paper (or on a flip chart) and ask your employee to name the scale, as in 'the scale of ...,' linking your employee's coaching goal to the scale. If your employee wants to become more self-confident, it would be 'the scale of self-confidence.' And if your employee wants to be more mindful, you can call it 'the scale of mindfulness.' It may take some time and effort to find the right word, but it is something you and your employee should do together.

1. Which words are you going to put at the start and end of the scale?

2. Where are you now on the scale?

3. Why are you not lower down on the scale?

4. What could you do to move up the scale?

Questions to ask someone who's unable to come up with options:

- Have you had similar emotions in the past and what helped you deal with those emotions?
- Are there people in your environment with similar emotions who do things that might be helpful in your situation as well?
- What is the most outrageous thing you could do?
- What would you recommend a friend do in this situation?

Figure 6.4   Scale Question

Scales that I have made with my employees in the past include the scale of assertiveness, the scale of boundaries, the scale of raising my profile, the scale of self-confidence, and the scale of decision making.

As soon as you have named the scale, ask your employee the following:
1. Which words are you going to put at the start and end of the scale?
If your employee wants to build up self-confidence, you will probably write 'insecure' at the left end of the scale and 'self-confident' at the opposite end.

Now ask the following Question:
2. Where are you now on the scale?
Have your employee rate himself or herself on the scale or point at a spot on the scale.

3. Why are you not lower down on the scale?
This question will get your employee to reflect on what he or she is already doing well or able to do.

4. What could you do to move up the scale?

This question forces your employee to think about how to get closer to the target end of the scale. Thinking in small steps makes changing more manageable. It makes it easier to oversee.

It can prove difficult for your employee to come up with actions that could help your employee change. If so, the following questions will help:

- Have you had similar emotions in the past and what helped you deal with those emotions?
- Are there people in your environment with similar emotions who do things that might be helpful in your situation as well?
- What is the most outrageous thing you could do?
- What would you recommend a friend do in this situation?

You can now, to wrap up the conversation, ask what your employee intends to do, and what you can agree on together. Next, ask when your employee would like to meet up again.

The scale question is a technique you can use as an alternative to the coaching matrix. Or you can use both in a coaching session or alternate them. Personally, I prefer not to use both during a single session, but it all depends on what feels best for you or what you think best matches your style.

Celebrating Successes

When planning to have a number of conversations with your employee about a coaching goal, you can start each session by asking about your employee's successes. In my coaching practices (as a coach or a manager), I go by a definition of success that differs slightly from what is usually considered a success. Normally, success is when you get something right or a hit a target. When you want to change, the first step to take is the step of awareness (see Figure 6.5). This is the step of looking down from your helicopter to see what works and what does not work. Therefore, in my view, a failed attempt to change also counts as a success. After all, it is all about what you learn from the failed attempt. If you consider both failed and successful attempts a success, your talk about changing is always off to a positive start. Your employee will then enjoy changing and not engage in a desperate pursuit of a specific end result. The thing is, therefore, for you as a coaching leader not to ask only about situations where everything went well, but also about what did not go so well. Tell your employee that you consider attempts that ultimately ended in failure also a form of success, simply because your employee tried something new. And perhaps something else did work out after that or will work out next time.

Gaining insight into personal beliefs that stand in the way of change - regardless of how irritating it can be to keep coming up against these beliefs - is the first step toward change. This is the insight that will help your employee get closer to the goal.

When asking about successes, it is important that you are clear in your questioning so that your employee tells you about actual changes your employee has made. I say this because it often happens that employees start listing successes that are basically 'flukes' rather than actual personal successes. Although it is nice that your employee has received unexpected help from a colleague, for example, or a compliment, it does not qualify as a success, because your employee did not do anything to achieve it. Calling something that you were already very good at a success does not work either. Only attempts to change behavior count, regardless of whether or not they were successful attempts.

When pursuing change, thinking in terms of successes will help you persevere when the going gets tough.

Awareness
Seeing what is happening

1. Recognition
   Hey, it happens (again)

2. Seeing a pattern
   This happens more often

Taking ownership
3. Action without result
   Trying something different (but failing)

4. Action with result
   Trying something different (and succeeding)

Note:
Others' satisfaction with you does not qualify as a personal success.
It is about you doing things differently.

Figure 6.5   Successes

When your employee self-effacingly says that 'it went okay,' ask about the details. Make it specific. 'What did you do differently to make it go well this time? What was it that made it a success?' Help your employee celebrate successes and reflect on successful attempts, no matter how small. Never leave successes uncelebrated!

Growth mindset

Professor Carol Dweck of Stanford University discovered that children have either a fixed mindset or a growth mindset. Children (and adults) with a fixed mindset are convinced that they have certain talents and that it is hard to learn new things. They say things such as, 'I just don't have great commercial skills' or 'Sure, I tried that once, but it's not for me.' They prefer to steer clear of any tasks they are not good at, so as to prevent negative feedback. Perfectionism or fear of failure can lead to someone being quick to give up.

People with a growth mindset, however, think they can get better at anything, as long as they try. They assume that skills are developed by trying and practicing, and that they will gradually get better at something. Someone with a growth mindset is able to learn from feedback or criticism.

It may sound very black-and-white, but it really isn't. The good news is that you can switch from a fixed to a growth mindset, purely by hearing or reading about it. The mere awareness of these different mindsets already sparks a change in your head. This in itself already means that you are thinking differently about growth and development.

To stimulate employees to develop their growth mindset, there are a few things you can do:

- tell your employees about the fixed and growth mindset (there are plenty of videos and articles online you can use)
- make sure your employees have experiences of success (when employees are assigned challenging tasks, they will experience growth and gain self-confidence)
- ensure a safe learning environment (let your employees know that it is okay to make mistakes and also share your own mistakes)
- talk to employees about the process (employees often have control over the process, but not over the end result)
- set a good example (it's a bit of a cliché, but like children who don't listen to their parents, but still copy their parents' behavior, employees often take more notice of what you do than of what you say. Show them that you are open to learning new things, that you pursue personal improvement as well, and that you see mistakes as learning opportunities)

Laura is not very good at following up on leads. During one of her performance reviews, I decided to bring this up. She told me that she feels apprehensive every time she has to call potential customers. She feels she is bothering them, and this makes her trip over her words. Basically, phone calls are not her thing, so she said. I decided to tell her about the growth mindset. We talked about how learning new things works, both in general and for her specifically. How making follow-up calls can be nerve-racking and how uncomfortable it feels when you have to do something you feel apprehensive about.

After talking to Laura about where these feelings come from and what would help her be more relaxed in these calls, she arrived at a solution herself. As it turned out, what she needed more than anything was to have one or two clear examples ready to give to potential customers, so as to actually feel confident about what she has to offer them. Although she still feels somewhat apprehensive, she decided to give it a go.

We agreed to talk again after she had done three calls. When we met again, she said that although she still doesn't like making these calls, she is managing to express herself better. And she even said that the calls are actually more fun than she thought.

Changing is Hard - The Learning Curve

Dating back to the 1970s, the learning curve (see Figure 6.6) shows how you go from unconscious incompetence to unconscious competence when learning a new skill. You may actually be in the learning curve yourself right now, having set out to be less of a mother to your employees. But so may your employee, who wants to be more assertive, work more meticulously, or become better at setting priorities.

- Phase 1: Unconscious Incompetence

Before you even know that you need to learn something, you are unconsciously incompetent. You lack a certain skill, but you are not aware of it. This phase does not affect you mentally at all, you feel fine. In fact, you may have felt fine yourself before you started reading this book. Everything's cool. And the same goes for your employee, as long as your employee is not aware of a personal development goal.

- Phase 2: Conscious Incompetence

But now, since you started reading this book, you may realize that there are things you need to learn. This is when you become consciously incompetent. Now you have a choice. You can choose to stay consciously incompetent (accept it) or you can choose to do something about it (change). This is the phase in which you may start to experiment, try something and explore the extent of the skill and how much practice you are going to need. You may, however, also feel that you will never succeed at acquiring this new skill. This will often make you feel bad.

And this is the uneasy feeling that your employee will have as soon as it becomes clear that you were right and that there is a development need. The fact that you have to work through this phase is what often makes changing so hard. You feel incompetent, and that is a feeling that most people want to get rid of as soon as possible. Deciding that 'this is just the way I am' can then be an easy way out, which is why some people abandon change processes at this stage.

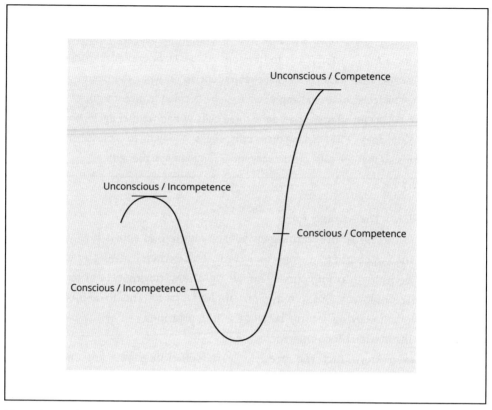

Figure 6.6   The Learning Curve

• Phase 3: Conscious Competence

After a while, you get the hang of the new skill, and the new behavior starts to come easier to you. You become consciously competent. This is a much nicer phase, because you are doing it, even though you have to do it consciously and think about it.

When helping your employee develop, this is the phase during which you need to celebrate successes. Although it may sound contradictory, attempts at behavior change that were ultimately not successful are still successes. It is all about becoming more aware. Together with your employee, look at what your employee is doing differently from before. But also look at what worked and what did not. Look for patterns together that will help your employee plan yet more new actions.

• Phase 4: Unconscious Competence

After some time and after a lot of practice, the new behavior finally seems to have become second nature. This is when you have become unconsciously competent. You can actually keep going through these phases, as you are likely to regularly discover new development needs. It is important to know that every learning process is made up of these phases. This model can help you understand why certain phases of the learning process feel so unpleasant, both for you and for the employee who is trying to change. This knowledge will perhaps enable you to be more understanding of your employee's learning process and make you realize why it can be uncomfortable for your employee when you point out yet another development need.

Useful Coaching Technique: Showing Functional Vulnerability

When you want employees to feel safe with you and confident to share their insecurities with you, there is no escaping it, you are going to have to show some vulnerability. Many managers find this difficult to do. They think they always have to exude an air of knowing everything and having no doubts, fearing they will not be taken seriously otherwise. Or thinking that if they let on that there is something they do not know, employees will question their legitimacy as a manager.

The fact of the matter is that showing vulnerability is not the same as being insecure. Showing vulnerability is not saying you do not know or are unable to do something, it is showing that you are human, with your own securities and insecurities, beliefs and doubts, strengths and weaknesses. It merely means that you not only show your successful, strong side, but also that other side of you.

Showing vulnerability means that you show that you are fallible too and do not know everything either. You take responsibility for your leadership role but are not afraid to honestly show that you do not have a monopoly on wisdom. By showing this side of yourself, your employee gets to know you better and you will ultimately build a much stronger working relationship. Employees will learn that they do not have to be perfect and certainly do not have to know everything.

A Little Getting Used to....

It may feel challenging and unnatural to do this, especially when you are not used to doing it. Perhaps you, too, have always believed that you have to be strong and know everything. The effect of only ever showing self-confidence is that employees also start to see you that way, as big and strong, and fearless. They may even admire you because of it, but ultimately it will make them feel small and less competent, because they do have doubts. And they will consequently be less likely to share these doubts with you. Chances are they will efface themselves and shirk responsibility, basically be less mature, and that they will increasingly ask you what to do. In the end, they will be more dependent on you and feel less self assured.

Another possible effect is that they start acting tough and only show their good side. As a result, they will never let you know what risks they have identified or what they consider challenging, they will only say what they think you want to hear. But what you want is for your employees to feel self-confident, take responsibility, and share with you what risks they have experienced. Openness breeds more openness.

Carry notices her employee Isaac looking rather nervous as he presents the annual plans to the MT. He stutters and fails to really engage with the MT, because he's so wrapped up in his papers and figures. Seeing that he is not coming across well as a result, Carry decides to talk to him afterwards to see if he would be willing to work on his presentation skills.

To put him at ease, she confesses to Isaac how nervous she felt at management team meetings at first. She tells him that she often felt insecure at these meetings and that this drove her to put even more time and effort into preparing for them. And that all that preparation did not improve her input at the meeting, because she became too rigid, and unable to present in the enthusiastic and engaging way she had envisioned.

By sharing all this with Isaac, she invites him to share his nerves as well, so that they can together explore what he can do to handle them differently. She could then coach him.

- Do you have any employees who would benefit from a coaching conversation (based on the coaching matrix) with you?
- What could be a potential pitfall for you during this conversation? Might you, for example, have a certain opinion on this employee's case, which could push you into the mother or macho role?
- Think back to last week, what are your successes? Try to identify both a successful and an unsuccessful attempt.
- How do you feel about showing vulnerability, does it come easily to you, or do you struggle with it?

6.4   Summary

In the coaching role, you encourage employees to find their own solutions and help them develop. A good coach is warm, open, honest, clear, sometimes confrontational, and shows empathy. It is a role of sitting back and asking questions, making your employee aware of his or her behavior and thought patterns, inspiring the self-confidence your employee needs to take the required steps toward achieving a goal.

You can use the coaching role when dealing with 'walk-ins,' employees who come into your office without a clear question, query, or need. Having adopted the mature mindset, you know that employees are responsible for their own tasks, health, and job satisfaction. Employees are perfectly capable of solving their own problems. It will save you a lot of time and energy if you manage to switch walk-ins to action mode by asking them right away what exactly they want from you.

Sometimes, you want to help an employee change, but this employee does not know yet that change is needed. When you try to start coaching without the other knowing it and wanting you to, which I refer to as coaching an unaware coachee, chances of success are virtually nil. And it will be very tiring for you. To make sure your goal also becomes your employee's goal, begin with respectful confrontation. Communicate what you have seen and what you would want to see.

If your employee still resists after this explanation, or is not excited about it, you can use the carrot or the stick. Use the carrot to entice, or the stick to scare by outlining the consequences of not changing. If all else fails, there are three things you can do: trick your employee into changing, execute the consequences, or simply accept that your employee will not change. You decide what is acceptable.

When an employee has a learning goal or a development drive, you can start using the coaching mindset. Trust your employee to be competent enough to autonomously take steps toward the goal. Coaching does not mean telling your employee what to do, but rather asking coaching questions, to get your employee to become aware of what is standing in the way of the target situation and what steps to take. It is about making your employee believe in his or her own capacity to analyze the problem and what to do about it.

A handy tool to use when having a coaching session is the coaching matrix. The first step in this matrix is to ask about the facts, about what your employee is grappling with. Next, you move on to your employee's emotions and the why of the problem. And then you ask your employee how he or she would like to feel. Finally, ask about the options and what your employee would like to do.

Start every conversation about changing by asking about successes, about what your employee has already approached or done differently. This will help your employee see things from different perspectives and stay engaged with the change process.

7   Reflexes

Having read the previous chapters, you might now think, 'Sure, I get all of that, but I often struggle to put it all in practice.' You know very well that you should not be judgmental, that you should call your employees to account on their behavior or results, that you have to represent the values of your company, but you often don't do any of these things.

> During leadership training, Tanya, a young manager, learns the steps to take in a difficult conversation where you have to deliver bad news (deliver the blow, let it sink in, and then take the next steps). In a role-play exercise with an actor she does very well. But in real life, at work, she notices that she does start to beat around the bush. She knows exactly what she needs to do and how to do it, but something is holding her back.
>
> Max, another manager, knows that he needs to give his employees more space and self-confidence, but it just makes him nervous. He is afraid of his employees making mistakes, and that it will then be up to him to rectify these mistakes. Time and time again, he double-checks his employees' work and takes responsibility away from employees by doing things himself.

In short, having the required knowledge and skills does not guarantee that you will actually be able to put them in practice. To achieve behavioral change, you first need the right knowledge and skills on how to make change happen. People sometimes need no more than that to set the change process in motion. Sometimes, you know what to do, but you sense a threshold or something blocking you. This is your beliefs kicking in, on the learning level where your reflexes take over sometimes.

The different learning levels are as follows:
1. behavior
2. skills, knowledge
3. beliefs, reflexes

Imagine you want to learn new behavior (level 1). Let's say you want to be more effective in how you deliver bad news. You want to be able to come straight out with the message and be less of a mole. First, though, you need to know *how* to do that. In the example, manager Tanya took training where she learned the theory and practiced it on an actor. She acquired the knowledge by learning the theory. And she acquired skills by practicing delivering bad news in a mock conversation with an actor (level 2). And yet, when she had to do it for real, she could not do it the way she had envisioned.

This is due to beliefs (level 3). Beliefs are certain values, standards, or requirements you have for yourself or others. For example: you have to be nice, you have to be perfect at everything, others have to treat you fairly. These beliefs, which are basically standards you set for yourself and others, outweigh the skills you have acquired.

> One of Tanya's personal standards is that she must be nice and not hurt people's feelings. When she has to deliver bad news, this standard (belief) interferes as a reflex, obstructing her from doing what she should be doing, which is to deliver the blow, and making her do what the reflex tells her to do, which is to be nice and kind to the other.

When you want to help your employees change, always bear these learning levels in mind. Start with skills, knowledge, and actions. This is often how behavior changes. If not, because reflexes take over, it is key that you zoom in on the roots of these reflexes. So, if your employee knows how and when to say 'no,' but repeatedly fails to say 'no,' you know you should look at your employee's beliefs to help your employee get ahead.

7.1 What Are Reflexes?

Everyone has reflexes to some degree. They regularly make your behavior less effective. They curtail your freedom of choice. In the following, I will go over a number of common reflexes of managers. But first I need to go into what reflexes are.

Reflexes are behavioral patterns that you have grown into and which are therefore very familiar. They start early in life, helping you hold your own in the world. For example: if you are always cheerful, you will attract positive attention. Or if don't make trouble, you won't get into trouble. But it can also be a decision you make at a certain point in your life. A decision, for example, to no longer trust people, or that you had better do things yourself to make sure they are done right. These reflexes or beliefs helped you at the time, but they still kick in sometimes, also in situations where they hinder rather than help.

In leadership, you need to be very aware of your reflexes and be able to control them. There are several common intervention reflexes that may take over. When they do, you are not doing what you had set out to do. Despite all the reading and learning about how delegating work to an employee with low task maturity will help the employee mature, you instantly think about how it would also mean relinquishing control. And you do not want to relinquish control! This is when your reflex stands in the way of you adopting your desired leadership style. After outlining some of the most common intervention reflexes, I will also list several exceptions, situations where it is actually useful to intervene (Section 7.3).

Appreciation Junkie

As the term suggest, appreciation junkies want appreciation, they just cannot get enough of it. Appreciation junkies want people to think they are skilled, fun, nice, smart, and strong.

The pitfall for managers who have this intervention reflex is that they take over from their employees because they want to be liked. Appreciation junkies duck difficult conversations because they are afraid employees will cease to like them. And appreciation junkies are not clear about their boundaries either. To please employees, they solve things for them. They will not confront employees when things get out of hand, because that is far too challenging for them.

> Jack has an employee, called Sophie, who regularly fails to complete her tasks. She is a tad messy and chaotic and doesn't get her work done on time. Jack knows that he needs to talk to Sophie about this. In fact, he's even practiced it during Coaching Leadership training. He knows what to say, but every time he plans to talk to her about it, the appreciation junkie emerges, telling him to be nice, and not hurt anyone's feelings. And so he keeps avoiding that difficult conversation with Sophie.

Perfectionist

Perfectionists want everything to be done to perfection, and preferably be perfect themselves as well. Perfectionists think, 'Things need to be perfect, and there is a better chance of them being perfect when I do them myself. If I take my eye off the ball, things will not be perfect.' Managers who are prone to succumb to this intervention reflex are at risk of stepping into the pitfalls of doing their employees' work for them, intervening out of a kind of fear that the work will otherwise not be done to perfection. Sometimes they lose themselves in detail, turning into micro-managers. They prefer to do it all themselves.

Natalie and her employee JP have agreed for JP to take a number of projects off her plate. Natalie has firmly resolved to give JP the space he needs, knowing that employees will only take responsibility if you give them responsibility to take. After a few weeks, she checks in with JP to see the schedule he has made for his projects. Looking at the schedule, she notices that JP has forgotten to include a few things. And although she knows it's not the right thing to do, she gives in to the perfectionist in her and adds the missing parts to the schedule.

Whatever

Someone with a whatever mentality has an aversion to difficult situations. They do not want things to be overly exerting or believe things will not work out anyway. It does not take much for them to find it all too much fuss.

Managers who are this way inclined might walk into the following pitfalls. They fail to confront their employees, because that is too much hassle. But they also intervene, because they consider coaching leadership far too time-consuming. Instead of taking some time to talk to an employee who has made a mistake, managers with this whatever reflex intervene immediately and take over from their employee, simply because that comes easier to them.

Janet is the manager of an employee whom she knows underperforms. At every performance review, she realizes that she would much prefer just to replace him. But she can only do that by first building up a comprehensive case to substantiate such a move, or by at least giving him a low score on his review. But again, she would then need solidly grounded reasoning of why she considers his performance below par. And this is all simply too much hassle for her. She would have to give specific examples and probably even engage with him about it as well. So, she just thinks, 'whatever,' and says and does nothing.

Moralist

Moralists have clear morals, an opinion, personal beliefs. A moralist thinks, 'My employee must do things the way I do them, or the way I think they should be done, because that's how they're done.' Moralists are full of judgment. Managers with a strong moralist element to their personality will come up against the following pitfalls. They will intervene and criticize based on the judgment. They make assumptions and are often critical. They are quick to conclude that things are not done the way they are supposed to be done, or that employees should change.

Bridget has an employee on her team, called Alex, who tells her that he's having difficulty coping with the workload. Bridget actually thinks his workload is not that bad. And personally, she is not one to complain. She was always taught to cut the chit chat and get to work. When the going gets tough, Bridget gets going. In fact, she likes a little bit of pressure, it boosts her performance. When Alex comes to her to talk about the stress he is experiencing, Bridget notices that she simply cannot get herself to listen to him. Even though she has learned all about how to be a more coaching leader and adopt an empathic listening attitude toward her employees, the moralist in her makes her cut the conversation short and tell Alex that everyone's busy and that no one ever died from a bit of pressure at work.

Controller

Controllers want control. They are convinced that they can only feel good when they know for sure that everything will be okay. They are continuously looking for certainty and ways to keep a grip on everything around them. Managers with this intervention reflex cannot let go and they tend to do everything themselves. They struggle to delegate tasks, worried as they are by the prospect of not being in control when letting an employee handle something. Controllers also find it hard to ask employees to come up with solutions, because it would mean relinquishing influence over the solution.

Ann knows that she has a tendency to intervene in her employees' tasks. During a coaching course she took recently, she became aware of how, as a child, she had learned to always want to be in control. Lack of certainty makes her restless, and she can only relax when she feels she's in control. During a session with her coach, they talk about Ann letting her employee Mary do more tasks autonomously. Mary is sufficiently experienced and wants to grow. But just before Ann goes on vacation, she gets stressed. Although she knows that it will help Mary's development to delegate work to her, she still decides to leave her phone on and check her email while on vacation. She is unable to suppress the controller in her head who tells her that things will fall to pieces if she doesn't do them herself.

Self-Doubter

Self-doubters consider themselves incompetent. They lack faith in their ability to complete a certain task. In fact, they know for sure that they will not be able to do it. Managers with a propensity to show this intervention reflex will criticize themselves and look only at what they cannot do, and what others can do. They will therefore often not even start something, thinking they will fail anyway. As a result, they tend to avoid coaching sessions with employees, believing that they will not be any good at it. Instead, they will just intervene and fail to get employees to take responsibility.

Meera tells her manager Andrew that she is struggling with a fear of failure. She is soon up for an important exam that she needs to pass, and she is losing sleep over it. She tells her manager at length about the tension she feels as a result. Andrew is taken aback by it. He's just completed training and learned how to use the scale question as a tool in a coaching conversation. But he doubts his ability to do it well. He is convinced he would fail if he were to try to coach Meera, and so he quickly gives her a few learning tips and sends her on her way.

7.3   Intervention as a Choice Instead of a Reflex

There you have it, no matter how well you have got the coaching theory down, your reflexes will sometimes be stronger than your rational thinking. In Section 7.4, I will go into what you can do to rein in these reflexes. But first I will present a few exceptions, situations where you, as the manager, actually have to intervene. This is when intervening is not a reflex, but a conscious choice:

- FIRE! There can situations that are truly an emergency that requires immediate action. For example, when something very important needs to be organized within a very short time span, you can step in and organize it. But do realize that if you find yourself stepping in too often, it is actually a reflex you need to work on.
- Panic. An employee can be genuinely upset about something, because something really horrible has happened, or because the employee is on the verge of a burn-out. In such a situation, you can make a conscious choice to take some work off this employee's plate for a while, relieving this employee of responsibility. If it happens often, however, you will have to confront your employee with it.

As you have seen, reflexes can really get in the way. They regularly keep you from doing something that you DO WANT to do. Awareness of your reflexes will enable you to separate yourself from them. One helpful way to look at your reflexes is to consider them a part of you. They are simply part of who you are, but you are not under an obligation to always do exactly what that part of you wants. After all, there is more to you than just your reflexes. Even when you realize that you are an appreciation junkie, you can still keep your eyes on your objective, on that dot on the horizon.

Let's say your objective is to be a clear, honest leader to your employees. You are fully aware of the appreciation junkie part of you, which is afraid of your employees not liking you anymore when you tell them that you expected more from their efforts. To still do what you had set out to do, while keeping your appreciation junkie reflex in check, you can try to take the following steps:

Step 1: Observe and identify
It will be helpful to teach yourself to reflect on conversations by writing down, for example, when you notice a reflex well up inside you. As soon as you feel one of the common reflexes coming on (or a reflex that resembles one of these reflexes), name it. The nickname alone will help you see the reflex as something that is a part of you, instead of something that you are. In fact, the nickname may even make it funny and therefore more light-hearted ('Oh, there's that controller again!' or 'Hey, that's the moralist talking'). Just consider it a sub-personality of yours, one that takes over sometimes.

Step 2: Look on, and do not give in
This is a very difficult step. You feel your reflex coming on, you realize what your reflex wants to make you do, but you stand firm. You look on and decide otherwise. You choose. You choose new behavior instead of your automated reflex.

Step 3: Go for your goal, not for your reflex
By keeping your goal in mind, you stay focused on what is the right thing to do. You stay focused on what you want to achieve with this new behavior, and on what it will bring.

Looking at your reflexes from a distance is what psychologists refer to as defusion, the opposite of fusion. Defusing your reflexes means to separate yourself from them. Your reflexes are not who you are, they are something you have. And you realize that you sometimes feel that you have 'fused' with your reflexes, as if you had no choice and your behavior was fully automated. The three steps above will help you step back from these reflexes, and to look at them and make a conscious choice between doing what you always do and trying something new.

Sam knows that he's a rather impatient person. Whenever he has asked an employee to do something for him, and Sam feels the employee fails to do it quickly enough, he is likely to say something along the lines of, 'Never mind, I'll do it myself.'

During Coaching Leadership training, Sam realizes that his mother always used to do exactly the same thing when he was a child. Ever since that training session, Sam has been recognizing the pattern. He now uses the nickname Speedy to refer to the part in him that is so quick to get impatient and wants to take over. As soon as he feels this impatience well up, he recognizes it and says, 'Stay down Speedy, don't get involved.' And he then chooses to hold back and only ask his employee for a status update.

- Which reflex(es) do you recognize in yourself?
- In what kind of situation do these reflexes get in the way of your effectiveness?
- What can you do, what steps are you going to take to be more effective?

7.5   Summary

Knowing very well and understanding that the mature mindset is the best way to give your employees responsibility does not automatically mean that you are always successful in doing so. Certain reflexes can get in the way. You might have one of the common intervention reflexes, such as the appreciation junkie, the moralist, the self-doubter, the whatever, or the controller.

These reflexes were formed during your childhood. They are survival strategies that help you handle difficult situations. These strategies then become automatisms that make that you often display the same behavior, without consciously choosing to. These reflexes stand in the way of you staying in the mature mindset. Given that they are automatisms, it is hard to unlearn them.

You can deal with your reflexes by taking these three steps:

1. see which reflex takes over and give it a nickname
2. look at the reflex and resist giving in to the reflex in how you react
3. keep your eyes on the goal and do what you choose to do, instead of what your reflex tells you to do

In certain situations, however, intervening is actually a good thing. When you consciously choose to take responsibility away from your employee, it is not a reflex, but a mature intervention.

8   Tricky Situations

Having read all about the pitfalls and reflexes, and about the different conversation techniques, you know all there is to know about coaching leadership. You know exactly what you can do to get the most out of your employees, and how to prevent energy wastage.

But ... sometimes your employees' behavior puts you in a tricky predicament. To help you get out these predicaments, I have included this chapter. Consider it a kind of FAQ list, withAnswers drawn from the personal experiences of managers who took my training courses, always accompanied by an example and a description of the potential pitfalls. I will also indicate in each case what you can do to make your response as mature as possible.

Before we delve into these tricky situations, allow me to briefly go into how behavior triggers behavior. To do so, please follow me into one of the components of Transactional Analysis.

8.1   Transactional Analysis

Transaction Analysis, or TA, is a theory of personality and a psychotherapeutic treatment method (see Figure 8.1). Developed by Eric Berne in the 1950s, TA differentiates three ego states a person can find themselves in: parent state, adult state, and child state. TA defines these three states as internal states and as states in interaction with others, where Berne means that when communicating with someone, both parties adopt one of the five positions shown in the figure below. The position that one of the two parties adopts has an effect on what position the other adopts, and vice versa.

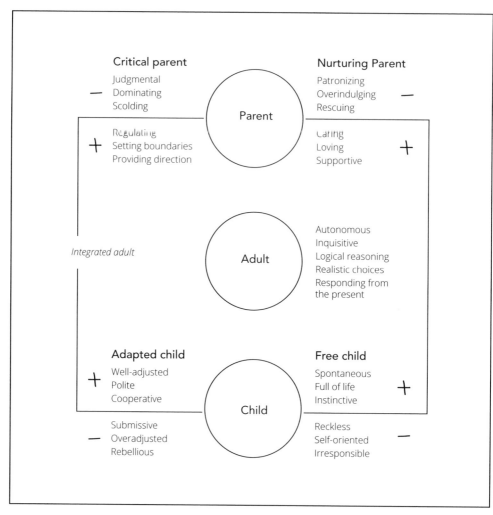

Figure 8.1   Transactional Analysis

Critical Parent and Nurturing Parent

The parent state can be subdivided into two subtypes, the critical parent and the nurturing parent. There is both a positive functional side and a negative dysfunctional side to each subtype. A healthy critical parent sets boundaries, regulates and provides direction. This is a well-known role for managers. Still, you can also overdo it as a critical parent, meaning that you become judgmental, dominant, and start scolding the other. The nurturing parent is caring and supportive. If you are a manager who wants to be there for your employees, you will undoubtedly recognize this role. But a nurturing parent who overdoes it will be patronizing, overindulgent, and take responsibility away from the other.

Adult

The adult state is a reflective state, communicating with the other from a position of equals, catering to both one's own and the other's needs. This is when you are not making yourself more important than the other, but not less important either. It allows you to engage with the other, while also staying within your boundaries (in the Mature Model: mature).

Free Child and Adapted Child

The child state can also be split up into two subtypes, the free child and the adapted child. And these subtypes, too, have a healthy and an excessive version. A healthy free child is spontaneous and full of life. In this child state, you simply do what you feel like doing and feel free to do it. But if you take it too far (and overuse free child behavior), you become reckless, self-oriented, and irresponsible. You shirk responsibility and think, 'I don't feel like having this difficult conversation.'

The adapted child is well-adjusted, polite, and cooperative, but an excessively adapted child is submissive and overadjusted. When an adapted child veers into the dark side, it can become rebellious and vindictive. This child role also shirks responsibility and thinks, 'It's not up to me to say something about this.'

8.2   TA in Interaction

Some of the states from the TA model trigger other states (see Figure 8.2). For example, if one of your employees talks to you from a child state, you will quickly be inclined to adopt the parent state.

If this employee asks what you would do in a certain situation (adapted child), you will be likely to respond, 'Well, I'd do it as follows' (nurturing parent) or 'How is it even possible that you still don't know this?' (critical parent).

Or your employee might say, 'I'm not going to do that schedule, no one even looked at it last week' (rebellious child, which means an overadjusted child). To which you will probably reply, 'Don't worry about it, I'll take a look at it' (nurturing parent) or 'Remember that you are making that schedule for yourself as well!' (critical parent).

If an employee engages with you from a child state, you will be inclined to respond from a parent state. Still, it might be you who starts from a parent state, because you criticize your employee (critical parent) or try to help your employee with something (nurturing parent), making your employee insecure and even afraid (adapted child). These common combinations of roles are called bonding patterns. Parent-child is one such bonding pattern, as is the adult-adult relationship.

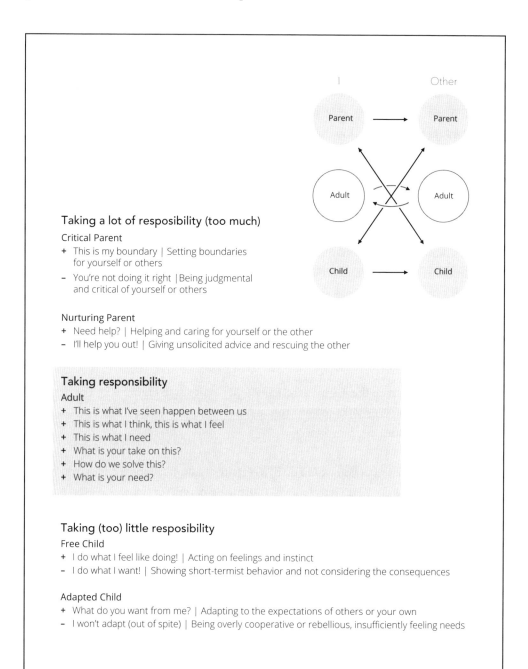

Taking a lot of resposibility (too much)

Critical Parent
+ This is my boundary | Setting boundaries for yourself or others
− You're not doing it right |Being judgmental and critical of yourself or others

Nurturing Parent
+ Need help? | Helping and caring for yourself or the other
− I'll help you out! | Giving unsolicited advice and rescuing the other

Taking responsibility

Adult
+ This is what I've seen happen between us
+ This is what I think, this is what I feel
+ This is what I need
+ What is your take on this?
+ How do we solve this?
+ What is your need?

Taking (too) little resposibility

Free Child
+ I do what I feel like doing! | Acting on feelings and instinct
− I do what I want! | Showing short-termist behavior and not considering the consequences

Adapted Child
+ What do you want from me? | Adapting to the expectations of others or your own
− I won't adapt (out of spite) | Being overly cooperative or rebellious, insufficiently feeling needs

Figure 8.2   TA in Interaction

If you want your employee to respond from an adult state, and therefore to take responsibility, your best bet is to use the adult role as your starting point. If you communicate as an adult and persevere in this role (even if your employee first slips into a parent or child role), chances are that your employee will ultimately also adopt an adult communication style.

What I think is great about the TA model is the given that there is always something you can do whenever you feel interaction with someone is not going smoothly. When you notice that you are slipping into the adapted child role when someone calls you out on something, you can - as long as you are mindful of it – switch to one of the four other roles from the TA model. You could even experiment to see what effect each role has on the other. There is always something you can do yourself to get out of a counterproductive pattern, and this will make you feel in control.

8.3 A Passive Employee

> During a performance review, you ask your employee about his ambitions and what development he wants to pursue. He fails to give you a clearAnswer. This is something you have seen in him before, this kind of passive attitude. You think that he may not be enjoying his job anymore.

Similar situations with the same pitfalls:
- an employee who shows little initiative
- an employee who claims to want a promotion, but does nothing to merit one
- an employee who only has a few years to go to retirement
- an employee who slouches a lot and never says a word at meetings
- an employee who has a reactive attitude, doing only what you ask, without ever going the extra mile

Pitfalls

Mother

You switch to action mode, taking on the responsibility yourself by suggesting possible development goals for him. One participant in my Coaching Leadership course even confessed that he once wrote an entire development plan for an employee, because the employee provided little to no input. This can be either mother behavior (I need to help him) or macho behavior (I'll do it myself).

Macho

You get irritated and criticize him, telling him what to do or giving the impression that you do not believe in it. You make plans for him, start managing based on task contents even more and monitoring him more closely, because you have lost faith in him. You may also have gotten tired of all the mothering, and therefore switch to the macho role.

Mole

You have had it with him, or you think 'whatever'. You simply stop addressing the behavior and just let it go. You are tired of having to work so hard at it (as a mother or a macho) and give up.

How to Handle It Maturely

Passive employees are asking for it. They take little to no responsibility, implicitly asking you to take responsibility. This is never an explicit request, but instead one communicated through their attitude. They are in a child state. The pitfalls of taking over loom large in this kind of situation.

A mature response means that you do not take responsibility away from your passive employee. Your initial response could be to adopt the child role, saying something along the lines of, 'Hmm, I don't know either.' Next, you can switch to respectful confrontation, confronting your employee with what you are experiencing, the effect it is having on you and what you would want to see happen. You could also grab the carrot or the stick from Section 6.2 to motivate your employee to be more active.

It is up to you to decide whether or not it is acceptable for your employee to not pursue any kind of development.

At some, generally young and rapidly growing, companies, I have seen that managers want everyone to keep growing and be super ambitious. But not everyone is intrinsically ambitious. In fact, it may be just as positive sometimes to have employees who are simply satisfied in their current job. The question is therefore whether it is acceptable for you or your company that your employee stays the way he or she is. After all, if you start to put in a lot of effort to get your employee to grow, you will be the one who gets tired, while your employee will not learn to take ownership of his or her own growth. This also goes for employees who only have a few years left to retirement. It is up to you to assess whether or not you can do anything about it. If you can, do it! Or would just accepting it be the best option?

What Else Could Be the Matter?

It is also always a good idea to see if you had a hand in propagating your employee's behavior. Might you have adopted the parent role too much and taken responsibility by doing the work for your employee or by constantly looking over your employee's shoulder? Other factors that could have made your employee passive:

- Your employee is angry about something and was never able to express this anger. And so your employee expresses it by adopting a passive attitude.
- Your employee has disengaged. Something has happened that made your employee decide not to worry about personal development anymore.
- Your employee never felt listened to. It can be work-related, but also a broader issue.
- Or your employee simply never learned to take initiative and doesn't know how to. A previous experience (at work) has accustomed your employee to lots of management control and little personal initiative.

8.4   A Defiant Employee

You want your team to get an effective team dynamic going and make sure everyone knows what to do, so as to prevent the same tasks being done twice by different team members. You have just heard for the umpteenth time that Tom failed to let Susan know what he was working on, so they are working on the same task. This kind of thing just drives you crazy, why won't they listen to you? You even addressed it at your last meeting, telling them that to be effective, they need to communicate to align their activities.

Similar situations with the same pitfalls:

- an employee who does not change (to a sufficient degree), even though he or she had committed to it
- an employee who keeps turning up for work late or makes lots of private calls at work, or who shows any other kind of behavior that you have already challenged

Pitfalls

Mother

You take over. As soon as you find out what Tom is planning to work on, you run it by Susan to make sure she's not working on the same thing, and vice versa. To prevent that the same task is done twice, you take on the communicator role to align your team members' activities.

Macho

Macho mode is the obvious choice here. In fact, there is already a macho tone to the example. You get worked up about it and call Tom out on his behavior, telling him that you've had enough of it, and ordering him to keep his fellow team members informed.

Mole

The whole thing has driven you to despair. You've talked to your team about it, you've tried to resolve the issue, but none of it worked, and so you slip into 'whatever' mode.

How to Handle It (Maturely)

Whenever an employee fails to stick to agreements, what you need to do is turn to respectful confrontation. Tell your employee what you have seen (specific behavior), what effect it is having on you, and that you would like to hear your employee's take on it. To truly understand the behavior, you need to assume a curious attitude to find out what drives the behavior.

If your employee still fails to change after this talk, or if you had already resorted to respectful confrontation previously, now is the time to give your employee an idea of the consequences of the behavior. If you have talked about your employee's lateness on several occasions already and you have already shown empathy by asking why, but your employee continues to be late for work, the only option that remains is to (consciously) go into macho mode and tell your employee what the consequences of this behavior will be.

What Else Could Be the Matter?

It is also always a good idea to see if you had a hand in propagating your employee's behavior. Reflect on your collaboration (from your helicopter position) and ask yourself if you actually made any mutual commitments as equals or if you came up with and imposed commitments. What could be the matter is that your employee could have a discipline issue or be such a perfectionist that he or she just freezes. Still, it could also be that your employee is angry with you and rebelling against you through passiveness.

> You have an employee who keeps moaning about everything and then some. About how he is only told about things when they have already been decided. About how he can't do his job properly, because he has no access to all the systems from home. Or about how he is unable to concentrate in the busy open-plan office.

Similar situations with the same pitfalls:
- an employee who always blames others or the situation
- an employee who bears a grudge (over decisions taken in the past, events that occurred a long time ago, sometimes even before you joined the company)
- an employee who always focuses on the negatives
- an employee who cries a lot or is just pathetic
- an employee who always claims to be entitled to all kinds of things (more leave, a company car, to go to conferences, etc.)
- an employee who gossips a lot and/or tells tall stories

Pitfalls

Mother

You want to help your moaning unhappy employee and think of all kinds of ways to get him to take a different view, trying to get him to change his mind. You feel responsible for how he feels and try to raise his spirits. Still, you do not take the moaning seriously, which will probably push him even deeper into his negative mindset, because he doesn't feel heard. It could also be that you start to nurture him, or better yet, unburden him by arranging things for him. 'Ah, how awful, let me check with the IT department to see if they can get you home access to the systems.'

Macho

Your employee's moaning bothers you, and so you tell him what to do. Like the mother, you try to get him to take a different view, saying things such as, 'That's just how those things go' or 'You can just prepare most of the work from home and then finish it at the office.'

Mole

The moaning annoys you, but you simply can't muster up the strength to bring it up again. You don't respond to it (anymore). Perhaps you did mother mode or macho mode first, but you may also have tuned out and slipped into mole mode right away.

How to Handle It (Maturely)

First of all, you can try to figure out whether it is due to your employee or due to you yourself that the moaning bothers you. Moaners make most people feel that there is something to be resolved, that they have to cheer up the moaner or change something for them. This makes people adopt the mother or macho role in response to a moaner. If you consider a moaner someone who moans without any kind of drive to find a solution, a moaner may not even be a problem. Could it be that you feel overly responsible when someone moans about something?

When facing a moaning employee, the most mature response is to first show empathy, taking the moaning seriously by taking your employee's perspective. If this is difficult for you, look at any aspect of the moaning that you can relate to. There must be some truth to it. Next, respectfully confront your employee with the behavior and the effect it is having on you. You could point out how much time your employee spends on moaning and that you tend to tune out during yet another lengthy moan.

You can also use the Control Model when dealing with a moaning employee. Go through the Control Model step by step with your employee (by showing Figure 2.2 or drawing it on a piece of paper). Link each step to your employee's moaning behavior and first look at the bottom part of the model: comparing, feeling bad, and the short-term response. Next, explain that if your employee wants to feel stronger or more powerful, there is a choice that can be made, as shown in the top part of the model. First recognize reality, and then choose to change, accept it, or leave. Ask your employee which of these three options seems the most appealing.

It can be quite a challenge to introduce this model in a light-hearted way, and not being too forceful in using it. If you are irritated, there is a risk that your attitude says that your employee *must* use the Control Model. This is likely to lead to resistance. I often make it light-hearted by saying something along the lines of, 'I've got this little model here that I'd like to show you. It's always worked very well for me to take this perspective, perhaps it'll be helpful for you as well.' It is a way of making light of it, presenting it merely as an option.

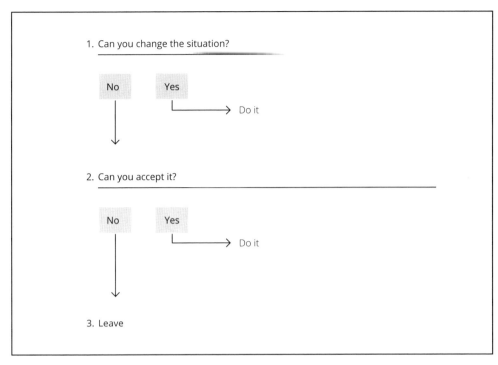

Figure 8.3   Clarifying Steps

The three steps from the Control Model can also be used on their own. If your employee has something on his or her mind or is annoyed with someone or something, and you notice that your employee struggles to take responsibility in the situation, you can also mention only these three steps (see Figure 8.3).

In a situation where your employee moans, you can ask your employee, 'Can you change the situation? If you can, do it!' If your employee thinks the situation cannot be changed, you can brainstorm together to see if the situation is indeed unchangeable. 'Is there really nothing you can change about the situation? If you cannot change it, can you accept the situation? If you can, accept it.' Again, you can help your employeeAnswer these questions. What kind of thoughts will help your employee accept the situation? And if your employee really cannot accept the situation, there is only one way left to take responsibility, by leaving. Exit the situation or physically leave. It may be odd to confront your employee in this way and to point out this option of leaving, but it does at least create clarity. And it helps your employee make a choice and take control.

What Else Could Be the Matter?

It is also always a good idea to see if you had a hand in propagating your employee's behavior. Have you tolerated the moaning for too long? Or did you fuel the moaning by moaning about something yourself as well?

A moaning employee feels ignored and unappreciated. When taking your employee's perspective, can you understand why your employee feels that way? Is there some level of truth to your employee's moaning? If you manage to sympathize with your employee's moaning, you may be able to do something about it by discussing it openly with your employee. You can tell your employee that you understand the discontent, but also that you would like to see a change.

- Other factors that could have prompted the moaning:
- Your employee may have been cut short once too often when moaning, feeling unheard and stepping up the moaning as a result.
- It could also be that your employee never learned how to solve something, how to be proactive.
- Or your employee may just be a general moaner in life and not know how to express himself or herself differently.

8.6   A Popular But Underachieving Employee

You have an employee who is not taking a certain aspect of his work very seriously. He is an incredibly upbeat guy, always joking around and very important in creating a good atmosphere at work. His fellow team members all like him, but the problem is that he never finishes his work. He is untidy and used to getting away with everything. When you try to talk to him about this, his response is rather frivolous.

Similar situations with the same pitfalls:

- a popular employee who does a good job, but sometimes goes too far in his or her behavior, making offensive jokes, being excessively chummy with interns
- an employee who is so popular that it has made him or her (perhaps unconsciously) the leader, an employee who sets the tone
- an employee who overestimates his or her own skills

Mother

The mother reflex is to go easy on your employee because you like him so much. You finish the work for him, or you are less critical of him than you are of others.

Macho

In macho mode, the frivolous attitude irritates you. If you keep that irritation to yourself, it will only grow and grow, and you might explode at one point.

Mole

It can be very tempting to just join in with the laughter and evade the conversation that needs to be had. After all, it is also fun to have someone on your team who is always happy and lifts the mood. Sometimes you get carried away in all the jolliness he creates.

How to Handle It (Maturely)

If your employee does not do his or her job properly, or there is something wrong with his or her behavior, the only way to change that is to respectfully confront your employee with it. Respectfully give your employee honest behavioral feedback (such as that you have noticed that your employee is not very serious about the work), what effect this is having on you (perhaps it makes you trust your employee less, monitor your employee more closely, or deny your employee certain assignments), and that you would really like to talk to your employee about it. After that, you can indicate what behavior you would like to see, so that your employee knows exactly what is expected.

What Else Could Be the Matter?

There can be different reasons that lead to a frivolous attitude. It may just be your employee's way to hide insecurity, or your employee may act this way to avoid being called out on anything. Perhaps your employee is not aware of this attitude (because no one ever pointed it out) and you are raising something in your feedback that your employee didn't know about himself or herself.

It could also be a case of self-overestimation, meaning that your employee really thinks he or she has made it and could even take over your job. And that while you think your employee would have to develop a few things first. Again, the only solution is respectful confrontation. It may be that none of your predecessors ever confronted this employee, because they all ducked that difficult conversation. Your employee's laughing it all off can also be passive-aggressive behavior because your employee is not taking something seriously.

8.7   A Poorly Performing Employee

> Your employee Ellis has been working at your company for quite some time. You recently became her manager and have noticed that she is not keeping up with all the changes. Her department needs to be more proactive instead of reactive. Ellis struggles to make this change and lags behind her co-workers. This issue has been raised with her on several occasions, but you don't see any improvement.

Similar situations with the same pitfalls:

- an employee who will be retiring soon and simply refuses to change
- an employee who has assignments that are beyond his or her capabilities
- an employee who really doesn't enjoy several essential tasks

Pitfalls

Mother
You start to go easy on her. Feeling with her or worrying about her ability to handle it, you take work off her plate and have others do it.

Macho
After a while, it irritates you so much that you start bitching about it. You criticize her and get angry.

Mole
Mole mode is also an obvious reflex here. This is when you avoid talking to her about the problem. You feel bad for her and dread the consequences, and so you choose not to honestly and clearly communicate your thoughts on the situation.

How to Handle It (Maturely)
When employees perform poorly, the only mature way of dealing with that is by just telling them to up their game. First have a good talk that includes respectful confrontation. Share your observations (of actual behavior) with your employee and tell your employee what effect the behavior is having on you. And most importantly, be clear on what you expect from your employee. If this does not produce the desired effect, you can use the carrot or the stick (Section 6.2) to activate your employee.

If all your attempts at motivating your employee have failed, what is left is the trichotomy of the clarifying steps from the Control Model: change, accept, or leave. If you have done everything you can to change your employee (talks, carrot, stick, coaching) and you cannot accept your employee's level of performance, you only have one option left. You are going to have to lay off your employee, which incidentally also means you are going to have to deliver bad news (Section 5.3). Conversely, if laying off your employee is not possible, for whatever reason, and changing is a non-starter, you have no choice but to accept the situation.

What Else Could Be the Matter?

It is not always straightforward to figure out why an employee underperforms. The main thing is to find out if it is anything to do with beliefs or skills. If your employee lacks the skills, you can look into how to get your employee to acquire these skills. You could then consider more detailed instruction, training, or a mentor. If dysfunctional beliefs are keeping your employee from doing a good job, even though your employee does know how to do a good job, coaching (by you as the manager or by an external coach) or personalized training might help your employee overcome the beliefs that are holding him or her back.

8.8   A Top-Performing Employee

> The ideal employee. He does his work very well and is pleasant to work with. You are confident that there is nothing you can't leave to him.

Pitfalls

Mother

What might happen is that you start helping him in pursuing personal development. You want the best for him, and so you think about possible career moves and plot a career path for him. Or you become overprotective of him, because you are so happy to have this fantastic employee, and you are even willing to overlook minor points of criticism.

Macho

You could start criticizing your employee because he fails to make major steps and is not committed to personal development.

Mole

The main risk in this case is that you do nothing. You think, 'As long as I don't hear anything, it's all good.' And you don't even mention it to him when (minor) things go wrong.

How to Handle It (Maturely)

Make sure the top performers on your team know that they are your top performers! It is key that you keep rewarding employees for their hard work and commitment, and not to abuse top performers. Remember to give your ideal employee plenty of compliments. A sincere compliment is more than just a 'well done' now and again. Explicitly mention what it is that your employee did that you thought was good and what effect it had. This will make it clear to your employee what you appreciate so much and why. Also mention possible minor points for improvement, so as not to deny your employee growth opportunities (and increase the chance of you getting irritated).

But beware, not everyone *wants* to develop. Some employees just want to work at a level where they feel comfortable for a while, without being challenged all the time. This may be temporary (triggered by circumstances in an employee's personal life) or your employee may just not be the ambitious type. Ask yourself if you can accept that. Perhaps you only want ambitious employees who want to keep growing. But also bear in mind that having a stable factor on your team, a senior employee that everyone can rely on, can also be very valuable.

What Else Could Be the Matter?

It could also be that your employee has become so good at his or her job that it has become second nature, so much so in fact that the job becomes boring. To prevent boredom, you need to check regularly whether your employee still finds sufficient satisfaction in the job. After all, you want your employee to stay this passionate and motivated. As I outlined in Section 2.1 on situational leadership, the risk that looms large with task-mature employees (M4: good at their job, and motivated and self-confident) is that the job becomes routine and they get bored. To prevent this from happening, regularly engage with your employee about the following:

- whether your employee still finds satisfaction in the job
- which tasks are particularly fulfilling?
- which tasks are less challenging?
- where your employee wants to be in six months', one year's, two years' time
- what skills your employee wants to develop, what tasks your employee would like to take on

Another risk for top performers is that they could suffer a burn-out. Due to the fact that they are overachievers who do more than others (because you subconsciously ask more of your top performers), they are at risk of doing too much and ending up in a situation where they feel structurally overworked.

8.9   A Sickly Employee

> Richard, one of your employees, is sick a lot. In fact, he stays home sick far too often. You suspect he may be overly quick to stay home sick and is not really sick in most cases.

Similar situations with the same pitfalls:
- an employee who calls in sick with what you feel are 'minor' discomforts such as a headache or a cough
- an employee with an unhealthy lifestyle
- an employee who claims not be able to handle any extra work

Pitfalls

Mother
When you start nurturing your sickly employee, you have slipped into the mother role. This is when you start suggesting solutions or advise him to do more exercise or eat healthy. Or you start to go easy on him, reducing his workload or even passing some of his tasks on to others. You switch to rescuer mode, wanting to solve the problem.

Macho
Your patience is bound to run out at some point. You become bad-tempered and start to criticize his reasons for staying home sick. This will be an unpleasant talk, as it will soon turn into an argument over whether or not your employee was really sick. A tug of war that will be utterly draining for you and may result in you making overly critical remarks.

Mole
If you go into mole mode, you will pull out of addressing your employee's frequent sickness absence.

How to Handle It (Maturely)

You can use the model for the frequent short-term sickness absence talk (see Figure 8.4). The line of action suggested by this model will prevent that you focus only on your employee's most recent absence (incident) and help you address the pattern (the fact that your employee stays home sick from work so often). Just like when delivering bad news, start with a clear statement of intent, saying that you want to talk about how to reduce the frequency of sickness absence. And you are not even talking about the sickness absence itself, you do not want to discuss whether or not your employee was truly sick. What you need to get across is that you think something might be up when someone stays home sick from work so frequently.

Essential: sickness absence perspective - what is your perspective on short-term frequent sickness absence?

1. **Preparation**
   - Announce the talk and subject (frequent short-term sickness absence)
   - Consult the employee's sickness absence record and take note of the reasons stated for each absence
   - Prepare the talk, if necessary

2. **The Talk: Introduction**
   - Get straight to the point: we are going to explore how to reduce the frequency of your sickness absence
   - When someone stays home sick from work so often, there must be something that is causes it (whatever that is)
   - Mature: hard on the issue, but soft on the relationship

3. **The Talk: Core**
   - Ask questions
   - Show understanding
   - Recap content and feelings
   - Active listening, let silences be
   - What can we do about it/what would you still be able to do when you stay home sick?

   Important: do not let the understanding steer you away from your goal

4. **The Talk: Close**
   - Work toward a solution or shared conclusion
   - Recap the talk
   - Make an appointment for a follow-up

5. **Document the Talk**
   - Make a report of the talk and have the employee sign it

Figure 8.4   Frequent Short-Term Sickness Absence Talk

Next, explore together with your employee if there is anything specific that is causing your employee to stay home sick so often. Use empathy to keep listening with curiosity. And use your mature mindset to prod your employee to come up with solutions.

What Else Could Be the Matter?

There could an infinite number of things wrong with an employee who is sick a lot. It may just have been a coincidence that your employee was sick several times over a relatively short period of time. But there may also be something else up:

- a serious health problem
- low resistance (temporarily)
- problems in the employee's private life
- problems at work (bullying, difficulties)
- excessive workload
- unhappy in the job (or bored)

By engaging with your employee in an open and interested way, you can try to identify the underlying issue.

8.10   A Stressed Employee

Your employee Olivia has been very busy for some time now. She doesn't look well and it is very clear that she is stressed. She is irritable at meetings with you and also with others. You also notice that she is a bit lost, she missed two appointments this week, and keeps dropping the ball. You are worried, afraid that it might get worse. You have asked her on several occasions if everything is okay, to which she replied that it'll get better once it has quietened down a bit.

Pitfalls

Mother

Not only managers, but co-workers also often behave like mothers when they worry about one of their own. You might say motherly things like, 'Are you OK?', 'Please take it easy,' 'Are you sleeping well?' and 'Are you taking good care of yourself?' Your employee will then probably reply by saying, 'Yeah, I'm fine, the worst of the heavy workload is nearly behind us.'

You might also do motherly things like doing tasks for your employee, going easy on your employee, shielding your employee from fuss, all out of a belief that you have to help your employee get through this.

Macho

You might also go macho, which often happens after you have spent some time in the mother role. If you have been trying to rescue your employee for some time, you are bound to get fed up with it, as you get irritated about how long your employee has been home sick and unavailable to you. You want your employee to do something about it.

Mole

You have all kinds of thoughts about the situation, but you are at a loss as to what to do about it. You have tried to offer help and be caring, so now you give up. Nothing you do seems to help.

How to Handle It (Maturely)

Expressing concerns about someone is generally something you do only when you see that an employee is having a tough time. But in most cases your concerns do not register. Whenever someone says to you, 'Are you doing OK?' how do you respond? I always think 'Yeah, it's all good, you just mind your own business, and I'll mind mine.' It always makes me a bit rebellious. It certainly does not make me take care of myself better.

What helps is confronting your employee in a genuine and respectful way, which means to say that you worry about your employee and that it is causing problems for you. In the case of the example, you could say to Olivia, 'I've seen that you've missed a few appointments lately and that you are curt with people. I know you're extremely busy. I worry about you and wonder if you're doing OK. And it is also causing me problems that you are making mistakes. I'd like to talk to you about how things are going and what you and I can do to improve your situation.'

Being straight with someone who is very stressed can be difficult. It feels as if you are not being nice. She is already stressed and then you also start telling her that it is causing you problems. Still, it is often the only way to help your employee break out of the situation. And it is the mature thing to do. After all, it is really creating problems for you, isn't it? And changing will also benefit your employee, to reduce the stress.

It is a bit like the stick method, as you try to make your employee realize that change is needed. As soon as you have got your employee to that point, you can deploy coaching techniques to explore together with your employee what is needed to reduce the stress. Make your employee responsible for his or her health and job satisfaction, and let your employee come up with solutions that will work for him or her.

Excessive Stress and Burn-Out

If your employee suffers excessive stress or a burn-out, consciously choose the mother role. This means you take over responsibility and give your employee room to recover. While recovering, your employee can rely on help from the company doctor, a therapist, or a coach. After a while, your employee can make a cautious return to work by gradually increasing the level of responsibility and taking on more tasks.

This process, however, is also one with pitfalls. To stay in your mature mindset, you need to be as frank as possible in discussing how you feel and asking your employee how he or she feels. Express your understanding (empathy) of the situation, but also point out that you want to know what to expect going forward.

8.11 An Emotional Employee

During a performance review with your employee you tell her that she's not up for a promotion. She starts to cry. You didn't expect that, so you try to explain yourself and console her. But you soon notice she's not really listening to you. In fact, her crying intensifies. She sobs about how hard she's worked and that she counted on a promotion. And about how unfair it is, because one of her co-workers did get a promotion, while he showed less growth, in her eyes anyway.

Similar situations with the same pitfalls:
- an employee who reacts angrily to being passed over for a promotion, not being assigned a project, etc.
- an employee who becomes unsettled when you share the details of a new project
- an employee who is visibly upset after a difficult meeting with a customer

Pitfalls

Mother
The example already has a bit of the mother role in it. You console your employee and try to make her feel better. You play it down by saying, 'Don't worry, you'll be in with a chance again next year.' Or you show so much sympathy and understand her pain so well that you also become outraged at her missing out on a promotion and ultimately tell her that she is right to be angry about it.

Macho

Perhaps you have little sympathy for crying co-workers, possibly because you would never cry at work. Or you may even feel that she does not even deserve a promotion. She counted on it, but what made her believe she was even in with a chance? This is responding to her emotions by being judgmental of her. You go against her, telling her that she could have easily seen this coming.

Mole

A mole response to emotions is to ignore the emotions. You keep talking as if the emotions are not there.

How to Handle It (Maturely)

Handling emotions is primarily a matter of acknowledging them and showing empathy (Section 6.1). It is important to allow your employee to express the feelings and experiences of the moment. Show that you understand, which is not the same as agreeing with your employee. When you show understanding, you are saying that you understand why your employee feels this way.

You can let your employee know that you feel with him or her by recapping the emotions you picked up on. This means not only recapping what your employee said, but also what feelings your employee expressed nonverbally. You can guess these feelings, it does not matter if you do not get it entirely right. Your employee will undoubtedly correct you and explain his or her real feelings. 'No, I wasn't angry, I was disappointed.' This will also help your employee settle down.

Don't

- Go against it
- Trivialize
- Generalize
- Soothe
- Join in with the outrage

Do

- Let your employee blow off steam
- Show understanding
- Recap emotions
- Ask questions
- Ask more questions

Figure 8.5   Handling Emotions

Follow this up with questions that tie in with what your employee is telling you, so that you get an idea of what made your employee so angry or sad. This way, responsibility stays with your employee and you give your employee the opportunity to bounce back unaided. This will also help you steer clear of the pitfall of trying to cheer up your employee and pull your employee out of this emotional state. When facing emotions, the thing is to not trivialize or try to soothe them, and not to engage in an argument over them. Instead, let your employee blow off steam and make sure your employee is allowed to show emotions.

What Else Could Be the Matter?
An emotional employee can have a minor or a major problem. Some people get emotional quicker than others. In a recent training course, one of the participating managers shared that she is one of those people who are quick to cry. But, so she pointed out, there is generally nothing to it, and she does not want co-workers to console her. Crying can also be a manifestation of anger. People sometimes show sadness when they are actually angry.

I know managers who have set themselves the standard of never crying at work. Whenever they see an employee cry, they are appalled and instantly judgmental. Therefore, be aware of your own views on showing emotions. And if you have trouble figuring out how to handle emotions, just ask your employee what to make of his or her emotions.
If your employee's fierce reaction is inconsistent with his or her normal calm demeanor, there is probably more up than you know. In that case, tell your employee that you were surprised by the heated reaction and ask if there is anything else the matter.

8.12 Quarreling Employees

Two employees on your team regularly clash with each other. Martin says that Esther never sticks to agreements, and Esther says that Martin is petty and shouldn't intervene in how she does her job. Martin is indeed very big on rules and rather strict. Esther, on the other hand, is more laid-back and gives her team more leeway. They are irritated by each other's approach.
At meetings, the tension between them regularly rises to unpleasant levels. This morning, Martin came into your office. He and Esther had a major argument over how to handle sickness absence, with Esther ultimately storming out. Martin asks you to talk to Esther about her behavior. He wants you to get her to act normal and stick to the rules.

Similar situations with the same pitfalls:

- employees who refuse to work together
- an employee who complains about another employee
- an employee who asks you to choose sides
- an employee who asks you to settle an argument
- an employee who asks you to talk to another employee about supposedly bothersome behavior

Pitfalls

Mother

The mother goes into troubleshooting mode, whitewashing the other's behavior. This is when you try to make them understand each other better. You say things like, 'Try taking whatever he says with a pinch of salt,' 'She doesn't mean it like that.' You choose sides. You mediate between your employees. In other words, you take over responsibility to try to solve the problem that exists between these two employees.

Macho

The macho denounces your employees' behavior and is irritated by their nagging. You feel they are just being childish, and you want them to just get on with their work.

Mole

The mole looks the other way, because it all seems far too complicated. You duck and think, 'Oh dear, I don't want to get mixed up in this.' You stay out of it and try to ignore the commotion out of a fear of sparking an even bigger conflict.

How to Handle It (Maturely)

For a mature response to a request for help, you need to know what help is requested. Ask your employee what exactly he or she wants from you, as that alone will already make your employee responsible for the solution. As soon as you know what your employee wants from you, you can decide whether or not you are willing to do it.

The best thing to do is to let your employees settle it themselves, telling them that you expect them to be able to work it out. You can approach your employee (or both) from a coaching mindset and talk about what is troubling your employee and how to carefully give feedback to the other quarreling party. You can even offer to practice this talk with your employee.

If your employees are really unable to work it out, or if they have already given each other feedback, you can decide to go into mother mode. You can ask someone to mediate or mediate yourself. When you sit your quarreling employees down, it is key that they both get the opportunity to properly formulate their feedback. You could choose to go through the coaching matrix with the both of them. Have them take turns to explain their view of the situation, how they feel and want to feel, and what actions they could take. This is a way of inviting both employees to express their preferences and needs instead of accusations.

Do not engage with each employee separately, as you would then still end up in either camp. If it is, or has turned into, a team problem, another option would be to get a professional team coach involved.

What Else Could Be the Matter?
There could be a power game hidden behind your employees' quarreling, because they (or one of them) could be trying to get you to pick one of them as the top dog. It is also always a good idea to see if you had a hand in propagating your employees' behavior. They could be clashing due to a difference of opinion caused by a lack of clarity in their respective roles and responsibilities. In that case, it is up to you as the manager to make it absolutely clear what everyone's responsibilities are.

8.13 Handling Your Own (Difficult) Manager

> Your own manager is not the leader you would like him to be. He has macho tendencies. He always knows best and has opinions about everything. He tells you exactly what you need to do and intervenes in all the details. You feel that you have to defend even the tiniest idea you have and that you barely get any leeway.

Similar situations with the same pitfalls:
- your manager is constantly in mother mode, very quick to take tasks away from you or give you tips on how to resolve something
- your manager is not up to speed with things or knows less than you
- your manager is never there for you, looks stressed, or cancels appointments
- your manager is not committed to your personal development, never asking you about it and not doing anything to help you
- your manager is not on top of things, makes mistakes sometimes

- your manager is clueless as to what it is you do, seems totally uninterested in your work, and so you can never turn to your manager for guidance
- your manager steals and takes credit for your ideas

Pitfalls

Mother

In some cases, you could actually slip into the mother role toward your manager. If you feel he is incompetent, for example, you may take responsibility by helping him with some suggestions, pointing out important things to bear in mind or even arranging things for him. When your manager is stressed, you might slip into the mother role in how you approach your manager.

Macho

You are bound to get tired of the mole or mother role after some time. When you do, it might just be game over as you switch to macho mode and become all judgmental and critical in your remarks.

Mole

The most common pitfall when dealing with a difficult manager is that you slip into mole mode. It is not easy to give your manager feedback and to openly and honestly share your observations and needs with your manager. It is easier to hope for the best and vent a little at home or to your co-workers. And you will probably become increasingly less proactive, less creative, less pronounced, because you have disengaged - you simply cannot muster up the strength anymore.

How to Handle It (Maturely)

As a manager, you are also responsible for your own duties, health, and job satisfaction. This is where the Control Model can help you out. To feel strong, it is important that you take responsibility. After all, your manager is not competent, attentive, or coaching. This is your reality, whether you like it or not. Can you change the situation? If you can, do it. You could use respectful confrontation on your manager. Tell your manager what you have seen, what effect it is having on you, and what change you would like to see. And then ask your manager whether he or she understands and is willing to change. If such a talk does not lead to change, your only remaining options are to accept it or to leave.

What Else Could Be the Matter?

It is also always a good idea to see if you had a hand in propagating your manager's behavior. Perhaps you have taken too little responsibility in certain areas. Or you may not have performed a certain task (correctly) or perhaps you keep putting it off. Could it be that you show resistance in response to certain tasks or you have kept your manager out of the loop? This is all childish behavior that can push your manager into the mother or macho role.

The opposite could also be the case, whereby you take on too much responsibility. You may even have patronized your manager or pretend to be much stronger than you are. This could make your manager feel that there is no scope to lead, manage, and coach you.

And finally, there could be issues that you have no knowledge of. Your manager may be under pressure from people higher up the hierarchy or have personal problems.

- Who is your most difficult employee, what kind of behavior does he or she display?
- Looking at yourself from the helicopter, can you see what it is that you do to perpetuate or even aggravate this behavior?
- What behavior does this employee display and how do you handle that?
- What could you do differently?
- What is the bottleneck for you? Respectful confrontation, finding out what causes the behavior, or communicating as equals?
- Do you take good care of/take responsibility for your own duties, job satisfaction, and health?

8.14   Summary

As a manager, you can run into all kinds of difficult situations. To handle these maturely, the common thread is that in virtually all cases, you need to:
- reflect (adopt the helicopter view of yourself and the other to analyze your part in making the interaction between you so difficult)
- confront respectfully (communicate the behavior you have seen, what effect it is having on you, and what you would want to see change)
- try to stay curious and figure out what causes your employee's behavior
- communicate as equals by taking care of both your employee and yourself, and by being clear and sincere, but also open and inquisitive

Bonus 1: The Truisms of No-Nonsense Leadership

1. To reflect = to learn

I firmly believe that you can only grow your personal effectiveness if you are able to reflect on your own actions and behavior. Only if you know yourself and are willing to change will you be able to become more effective. To become a better leader, it is therefore essential that you make time to reflect on yourself and on the other, that you look at your interaction from a distance, trying to objectively analyze what you are doing to perpetuate the situation and why. And finally, reflect on whether or not your actions are working. Especially when things do not go our way, we tend to look for someone or something to blame. This is the opposite of taking responsibility. Taking responsibility means that when things are not going your way, you look at what you could have done differently.

2. The Answer to most questions is 'let's talk about it'

As you read this book (or take one of NONONS' training courses), you may after a while get the idea that there is one single answer to all the questions presented here, and that is 'let's talk about it.' And you would be right. The most mature way of handling difficult situations is to talk about them in an open, honest, and respectful manner. No matter who it is who is causing you trouble or whatever you experience during a conversation, always make sure you step into your helicopter and look down. Examine what is going on with you and the other. Talk about it with the other as equals and find out how the other feels about it. Ideally, you should do this in the moment, as and when it happens.

3. If you have something to say, say it; if you have something to ask, ask it

When learning coaching skills, many managers start asking questions purely for the sake of asking questions. When challenging an employee on a poor job done in a recent project, they may ask questions such as, 'How did you think the project went?' This is not a question asked out of sincere interest, but a leading question. Your employee will sense that. Only ask questions when you need to know something. If you have something to say, such as that your employee performed poorly, tell your employee respectfully what you think, and tell your employee what you want.

4. If you work hard, the other won't have to

If you work hard, your employee won't have to. The more you do, the more you are rescuing and troubleshooting. The more you direct and organize, the less your employee will do any of those things. Giving employees responsibility really means dialing down your work rate. In practice, it means biting your tongue and sitting on your hands to rein in your intervention reflexes. If you manage it, you will soon see that it is your employee who has to get stuck in.

5. New behavior is acquired by doing, doing, and doing

When learning new behavior, it will take a while for it to become second nature. Consider your old behavior an interstate highway and your new behavior a dirt track. Even after you have traveled the dirt track a hundred times it will still not be as smooth as the interstate. In our Coaching Leadership courses, we therefore use exercises to have participants practice certain behavior routines. They practice respectful confrontation, delivering bad news, and the coaching session, and then they practice it again, and again. The main focus in these exercises is to have participants practice not solving things for employees. Participants always say they learned the most from all that practicing. Lots of practice also boosts the chances of the behavioral change being a permanent one. So, put your good intentions in practice. Just do it! And do it often. It doesn't matter if you're successful or not, it matters that you try. Or take training that includes lots of practice with this mindset, knowledge, and skill set. Enjoy!

Bonus 2: Glossary

Active Listening
The listening technique that consists of three skills: listen, recap, and keep asking questions. *Page 50.*

Appreciation Junkie
This reflex sees you do things for your employee and take over responsibility, as you crave appreciation and want to be liked. *Page 121.*

Bad News
It's the kind of talk you never want to have, but sometimes have to have. When delivering bad news, make sure you do it well: prepare, deliver the bad news right away, absorb the blow, and wait until your employee has assimilated it before you ask whether your employee wants to talk about what's next now or later. *Page 87.*

Change, Accept, Leave
When things are not going your way, take ownership. You always have the choice to change the situation, accept it or leave. *Page 55.*

Clarifying Steps / Taking Ownership
Not letting yourself be swept along helplessly, not moaning about a situation, neither about others nor about yourself. Making a conscious choice to change, accept, or leave... and acting accordingly. *Page 41 and 137.*

Coach Role
One of the roles of anyone in leadership is the coach role, which is the role that consists in encouraging employees to find their solutions themselves and helping employees develop. *Page 59 and 93.*

Coaching Matrix

This technique enables you to analyze the situation that is bothering your employee and get your employee to come up with solutions to the problem.
Page 105.

Coaching Mindset

A mature mindset, with a firm belief that others are responsible for their own duties, health, and job satisfaction. A coaching mindset means presenting yourself as an equal to your employees and supporting them. It is about getting employees to independently analyze their problems or take steps to solve them. *Page 12.*

Commit

To agree, at the start of a conversation, on what you are going to talk about. If you are both clear on that, the conversation will stay on track. And it will also prevent post-conversation frustration over a failure to discuss things that you really wanted to address. *Page 52. See also: sub-commitment*

Compliments

Tell your employees what you appreciate in them or in their behavior. Be generous with compliments, be honest and specific. *Page 83.*

Controller cdd

Controllers want to have everything under control. Managers with a controller reflex want to prevent errors at all cost by always wanting to know everything and monitoring things closely. *Page 123.*

Drama Triangle

This model from Transactional Analysis describes common behavior that stands in the way of effective communication and collaboration. Due to the fact that you have one role or multiple roles in this triangle – persecutor, rescuer, or victim – you and your employee basically engage in a sort of game. You can break out of this by switching to the winners triangle. *Page 29. See also: Transactional Analysis*

Empathy

Feeling with the other, but most of all allowing the other to feel whatever it is they feel. *Page 95.*

Fixed Mindset

A term coined by Professor Carol Dweck, describing the mindset of 'this is just the way I am,' effectively denying your own learning ability. *Page 121.*

Frequent Short-Term Sickness Absence Talk

When your employee is sick a few times in a row, you can use the model for the frequent short-term sickness absence talk. *Page 144.*

Growth mindset

Another term coined by Professor Carol Dweck, describing the mindset of believing that anyone can grow and that there is always scope for improvement. People with this mindset actually turn out to grow more/faster. *Page 121.*

Handling Emotions

When your employee gets very emotional the best way to handle that is acknowledging them and showing empathy. *Page 148.*

Helicopter

The perspective from which you look at yourself during self-reflection, or when you reflect on your interaction with the other or others. What do you see? What can you see yourself doing? What does the other do? What happens between you? This will help you talk about the process. *Page 48.*

Helper

A role in the winners triangle. You are not a rescuer with unsolicited advice who wants to solve the other's problems, but instead a helper who asks what the other needs, makes an offer, and does not take over responsibility. *Page 31.*

Leader Role

One of the three roles in leadership is that of leader. The leader conveys the mission, vision, and strategy, knows and shares company values, and motivates and inspires employees. *Page 59 and 63.*

Learning Curve

Changing is hard. You move through fases from unconscious incompetence to unconscious Competence. *Page 113.*

Listening (Listen, Recap and Keep Asking Questions)

These are the steps of active listening. *Page 50.*

Macho

Pitfall from the Mature Model. You know best, you are judgment or critical. You tell the other what to do or how something is done. *Page 19.*

Mother

The pitfall from the Mature Model where you believe that you have to take care of the other, or where you think you will be considered a nice person if you just lend a helping hand. This means that you take over responsibility. *Page 15.*

Manager Role

One of the three roles in leadership is that of manager. The manager translates vision to personal goals, monitors results and behavior, assesses and makes adjustments as and when necessary. *Page 59 and 73.*

Mature mindset

The mindset that believes that everyone is responsible for themselves. *Page 14.*

Mature Leadership

Leadership where you take responsibility for your job as manager. You believe that your employees are responsible for their own tasks, job satisfaction, and health. *Page 11.*

Mole

Pitfall from the Mature Model. You know that you need to do or say something, but you don't. You look the other way, because you are afraid of encountering resistance. You've given up, you simply don't feel like engaging. *Page 24.*

Moralist

Moralists want everything done by the book. Managers with a moralist reflex have a very clearly defined idea of how things should go. And they want their employees to adhere to that idea as well. *Page 122.*

Perfectionist

Perfectionists want everything done to perfection. Managers with a perfectionist reflex think results will be better when they do it themselves. Without their supervision, things will go wrong, or so they think. *Page 121.*

Reflexes

Even if you know very well what is the wise and effective thing to do, intervention reflexes can still make you act in the entirely opposite direction. These are old common reflexes, such as the perfectionist and appreciation junkie, which have been with you forever and make that you don't always do what you should do. This is because your obstructing dysfunctional beliefs are sometimes stronger than your capacity for reason. *Page 121.*

Respectful Confrontation

Our equality-based mature way of confronting someone with their behavior, so as to engage in conversation about it. Say what you have to say, without making yourself bigger or smaller than you are, and seeing that the other is not bigger or smaller than he or she is. The steps to take are to observe behavior, communicate the effect the behavior is having on you, and finally to communicate your request/need. *Page 75.*

Roles in Leadership

A leadership position is made up of three roles: the role of leader, the role of manager, and the role of coach. It is advisable to always make a conscious choice as to what role to use for a specific purpose. *Page 58.*

Scale Question

A practical coaching tool that asks your employee to choose a name for the scale and pinpoint his or her position on it. The next step is to have the employee select actions that will take him or her closer to the goal. *Page 108.*

Self-doubter

Self-doubters think they will fail anyway. Managers with a self-doubt reflex are so negative about themselves that they do not even consider having coaching sessions with their employees, because they think, 'I can't do it anyway, why bother?'. *Page 124.*

Silence

Silence is golden in coaching leadership, it is a quality of a good listener. Allow the other to find an answer or the right words. If the other doesn't have an answer ready, this probably means you asked a very good question, one that will produce insight. Give your employee some time to come up with an answer on his or her own. *Page 51.*

Situational Leadership

Adapting your leadership style to your employee's willingness and competence for a specific task. *Page 35.*

Staying in Control of the Conversation

Make mutual commitments at the start and during the conversation. Stay in the helicopter, monitor where the conversation is going and mention it when the conversation is getting difficult. *Page 52.*

Successes

In a coaching situation a success is not only something that went well but also something that did not go well. As long as you gain awareness about your beliefs and behavior. With that awareness you can take ownership. *Page 111.*

Transactional Analysis

A psychological theory on how people behave and communicate with each other. In Transactional Analysis, there are three basic states: parent, adult, and child. *Page 127.*

Values

Values are not the same as goals. They basically exist on a higher plane than goals. A goal is something you check off, while values are for life. To run a marathon can be one of your goals in life. A healthy lifestyle is a value. It is useful, and also fun, to think about what your personal goals are in life and in your work. Companies and organizations also have values. In the leader role, you are aware of these values and you share them with your team. *Page 65.*

Vulnerability

Functional vulnerability means being open about your own needs, thoughts, and feelings, creating a safe environment where your employee will also feel confident to share things. *Page 115.*

Walk-Ins

Someone who comes into your office out of the blue, saying 'Do you have a minute?' Or an employee who comes in with a long story but without a clear request. *Page 98.*

Whatever

The 'whatever' reflex is all about avoiding difficulty. Managers who have this reflex will try to get out of coaching sessions. *Page 122.*

Winners triangle

The much more engaging, practical, and effective version of the drama triangle where you treat each other as equals, from a mature mindset. When you get caught up in the drama triangle, try to break out of it and move into the winners triangle. It can be done. *Page 31*

Acknowledgments

I never thought I would see my name on a book cover. In fact, I was set up by my partner Anne de Jong. Here's how it went:

This book was initially a joint project of ours, but one day Anne told me that she wanted to dedicate all of her time to coaching. Coaching rather than leadership is her specialist area. Leadership is more my passion, combining the coaching mindset with leadership skills. And so she put the ball in my court. And even though a voice in the back of my head screamed, 'No, I can't write this book on my own,' my mouth bravely uttered the words, 'OK, I'll do it.' But I didn't tell anyone. I was far too scared I wouldn't pull it off. But when I posted a tiny message on LinkedIn about my writing this book, everything changed. Ever since I posted that message, I have been receiving suggestions and ideas from friends, family members, managers in my training courses, and even from people in the schoolyard at my children's school. In December, Anne and I spent three days in Bergen to give the entire structure of the book a thorough once-over. Therefore, these acknowledgments are first and foremost directed at Anne, without whom I would never have embarked on this adventure. And because my views on coaching leadership are based on her coaching expertise and ideas. So, Anne, you are not only the most fun, intelligent, and delightful partner and friend I could have wished for, you are also my guru and inspiration.

Needless to say, I also owe a great debt of gratitude to everyone I had the honor of managing. They are the ones who made leadership fun, sometimes difficult, but most of all memorable. Alongside my former co-workers, everyone who ever took part in one of my training courses, and my friends and their stories, they provided the inspiration for the many real-life examples in this book.

Naturally, a word of thanks also goes out to my dear NONONS co-workers, because they make my work worthwhile every day. Mieke, because I'd never have met Anne if it weren't for you. My exceptional friends, because they were already proud of me and wanted to order the book when it was no more than a table of contents.

Janet, I am extremely grateful to you for editing the book (and adding a humorous touch). Many thanks also go out to my positive and honest pre-readers Paul, Merle, Wilco, Anneke, Sophie, and Femke. And special thanks Wardy for all his support and advice to realize this English edition. And Tanya, Cliff, and Georgia, who helped Erwin and me put the finishing touches to the English translation. Words fail me to express how pleased I am that you helped me in this way.

Dear mom, from you I inherited the gift of being able to explain things clearly. A passion for learning and facilitating the learning of others. And a drive to figure out what makes people tick. And dad, you have passed your no-nonsense approach to life on to me (I miss you).

Dearest Paul, thank you for the space you give me. You've never stopped believing in me. My final word of thanks goes out to the two loveliest little persons on this planet, Teun and Eline, who are the most confronting and also the most beautiful mirrors there are.

Nadia van der Vlies
Amsterdam, April 2019
www.nonons.nl

Literature

Bakker, A. & J. Halmans (2014). *Coachen met lef. Waar Transactionele Analyse en Voice Dialogue elkaar versterken.* Amsterdam: Uitgeverij Boom Nelissen.

Brené Brown on Empathy: https://youtu.be/1Evwgu369Jw

Dweck, C. (2011). *Mindset, de weg naar een succesvol leven.* Amsterdam: SWP.

Harris, R. (2010). *Acceptance en commitmenttherapie in de praktijk. Een heldere en toegankelijke introductie op ACT.* Amsterdam: Hogrefe.

Hersey, P. (2011). *Situationeel leidinggeven* (25th edition). Amsterdam: Business Contact.

Hersey, P. & K.H. Blanchard (2007). *Management of Organizational Behavior (9th International Edition).* New York: Pearson.

IJzermans, T. & C. Dirkx (2013). *Beren op de weg, spinsels in je hoofd.* Zaltbommel: Thema.

Jong, A. de (2016). *No-nonsense coaching. Zelfverzekerd en effectief coachen.* Amsterdam: Boom.

Kouwenhoven, M. (2007). *Het handboek strategisch coachen.* Amsterdam: Boom.

O'Connor, J., J. Seymour & M. Stoltenkamp (2002). *NLP-gids voor optimaal functioneren.* Haarlem: De Toorts.

Rosenberg, M. (2011). *Geweldloze communicatie. Ontwapenend, doeltreffend en verbindend.* Rotterdam: Lemniscaat.

Stewart, I. & V. Joines (2010). *Transactionele Analyse, het handboek.* Amsterdam: SWP.

Visser, C. & G. Schlundt Bodien (2009). *Doen wat werkt. Oplossingsgericht werken, coachen en managen.* Culemborg: Van Duuren Management.

Vonk, R. (2014). *Je bent wat je doet. Van zelfkennis naar gedragsverandering.* Amsterdam: Maven.